TWAYNE'S WORLD AUTHORS SERIES

A Survey of the World's Literature

Sylvia E. Bowman, Indiana University

GENERAL EDITOR

INDIA

Mohan Lal Sharma, Slippery Rock State College

EDITOR

Rabindranath Tagore

TWAS 402

Rabindranath Tagore, Hampstead, London, 1912

RABINDRANATH TAGORE

By MARY M. LAGO

University of Missouri – Columbia

TWAYNE PUBLISHERS

A DIVISION OF G. K. HALL & CO., BOSTON

Library of Congress Cataloging in Publication Data

Lago, Mary M.
    Rabindranath Tagore.

    (Twayne's world authors series; TWAS 402: India)
    Bibliography: pp. 165–70
    Includes index.
    1. Tagore, Rabindranath, Sir, 1861–1941.
PK1725.L3   891'.44'14   [B]   76–9776
ISBN 0–8057–6242–6

For Alicia and Carlo Coppola
with thanks

Contents

About the Author

Mary M. Lago received her B.A. Degree from Bucknell University in 1940, and, in 1965 and 1969, her M.A. and Ph.D. Degrees from the University of Missouri—Columbia. She is Associate Professor of English at that University; her special interest is Late Victorian and Edwardian Literature. She is a translator of short stories and poems by Tagore and other modern Bengali writers, and author of articles and reviews on East-West literary exchange. Her work has appeared in *Beloit Poetry Journal, Books Abroad, Chicago Review, The Cornhill Magazine, East-West Review, Encounter, Hindustan Standard, Indian Literature, The Journal of Asian Studies, The Journal of Asian History, The Journal of South Asian Literature, Literature East and West, Pacific Affairs,* and *Studies in Short Fiction.* She is editor of *Imperfect Encounter: Letters of William Rothenstein and Rabindranath Tagore, 1911–1941;* senior editor of *Max and Will: William Rothenstein and Max Beerbohm, Their Friendship and Letters 1893–1945;* and editor of *Men and Memories,* a one-volume abridged edition of the three volumes of William Rothenstein's memoirs.

Preface

A study of Rabindranath Tagore as writer, as personality, and as a pervasive cultural force invites both the scholar and the general reader to consider the complexities, not only of one man's astonishing career, but of a vast and intricate network of intercultural relationships. Tagore's talents were so various, and his exercise of them so prolific and so influential, that to compress them into a relatively brief account is to risk leaving the reader with diffuse impressions that do the subject less than full justice. Tagore's international success, so sudden and so spectacular, gave rise to a whole spectrum of quite intense reactions to him and to his work, reactions that ranged from unquestioning adulation to impatience and disenchantment. These extremes have immensely complicated the task of re-assessment, and it is further shadowed by widespread unaware-ness of his cultural background and sources, his uses of these, and the effect of colonial status upon generations of Indian writers. To these disabilities must be added the ineptitude with which some of Tagore's most important works were trans-lated, the unsystematic manner of their presentation to non-Bengali readers, and the consequent difficulty, after the first great burst of popularity, of obtaining for him the second hearing that he deserves.

This study, therefore, concentrates upon consideration of repre-sentative works by Tagore as lyric poet and as writer of that modern prose form most nearly analogous to the lyric, the short story. Both genres are, by definition, brief and highly personal; both strive to create a single unified impression. Short fiction is a relative newcomer in Bengali literature, but the lyric poem and abundant evidence of an abiding Bengali affinity for this form of expression extend far into the past, to the dim origins of Bengal's cultural history. That no surname is needed in Bengal to further identify the poet Rabindranath is evidence of the extent to which he is master of idioms that are fundamental in Bengali life and thought. He is known also as, simply, *Kabi*: the Poet. First, last, and always he thought of himself as a poet. No matter how far-ranging his explorations and achievements, in philosophy, religion, educational and political theory, he returned always to the concept of himself as, in the most literal sense, a maker of songs. Whenever he was too long away from these, he felt that he had betrayed his true self. His own estimate of his vocation is here invoked, therefore, as justification for the limitations imposed upon the present study.

In the second place, it seems essential that discussion of Rabindranath's literary achievement be placed squarely in the context of the great changes in his life occasioned by the events of 1912 and 1913. These years comprise a turning point after which nothing was, or could have been, what it was before. He had always fought a relatively solitary battle with inner tensions of various kinds, but after 1913 and the award of the Nobel Prize for Literature, those tensions that may be used constructively to keep the writer alert and sensitive began instead to interfere more and more with sustained lyric creation. As the 1920's advanced, Tagore and the general public outside of India, which had known him first and best as a creator of lyric forms, fell increasingly out of touch with each other.

Finally, one must bear in mind that general public's lack of curiosity about what lay beneath the appearance of serenity that was so great a part of Tagore's appeal. This lack of curiosity, which always threatened to harden into antipathy, in one instance after another appears in the guise of complacency about imperial relations. This incipient alienation worked in both directions: Rabindranath, whose capacity and opportunities for neutralizing the old imperial stereotypes surpassed those of any other Indian writer of modern times, often failed to perceive, until it was too late, that his affairs unduly burdened some of his most valuable friends and associates in the West. The consequent weakening of his international ties hampered the delicate processes of translation, and this in turn snapped that most crucial link between a writer and his international audience. The present study is literary, not socio-historical, but all of these extra-literary concerns are inescapable parts of the picture: allusions in the text and some bibliographical entries will indicate their importance for Tagore's career in particular, and for East-West literary relations in general.

This study relies chiefly upon Tagore's works available in English translation, although some untranslated Bengali works will be referred to from time to time, not only to convey some sense of the richness of the Bengali tradition, but also as an invitation to the learning of a beautiful and rewarding language. The two central chapters deal with Tagore as lyric poet and as writer of short fiction. Although the works discussed under various subheadings in these chapters are generally considered in the order of their composition, the order of their selection after 1912 for non-Bengali audiences was on the whole so unchronological that discussion of these has been organized according to themes and techniques that dominate Tagore's work in each genre.

Above all, it is hoped that this book may help to mend and to strengthen old ties, by presenting Tagore in his own favored voice as lyricist, and by suggesting a perspective from which to view the national and the international aspects of his long and distinguished career.

MARY M. LAGO

May 1975
Columbia, Missouri

Acknowledgments

I wish to thank the Trustee for the Estate of Rabindranath Tagore, for permission to quote from published and untranslated works and from unpublished letters of Tagore. For permission to quote from published works of Tagore, I should like to acknowledge approval by Asia Publishing House, The Macmillan Company Ltd., London; Visva-Bharati Publications, Calcutta; New American Library; University of Missouri Press; and Harvard University Press, for material © 1972 by the President and Fellows of Harvard College. I wish further to acknowledge permission from the following, for quotations from various published works: Mrs. Pratibha Bose for Buddhadeva Bose, *An Acre of Green Grass* and *Tagore: Portrait of a Poet*; Bookland Private Ltd., Calcutta, for Sujit Mukherjee, *Passage to America*; Thomas Y. Crowell Co., New York, for Frank O'Connor, *The Lonely Voice*; Krishna Kripalani, for *Rabindranath Tagore*; The Macmillan Company Ltd., London, for Ernest Rhys, *Rabindranath Tagore: A Biographical Study*, for Edward J. Thompson, *Rabindranath Tagore: Poet and Dramatist*, and for a letter of W. B. Yeats, from *Letters to Macmillan*, edited by Simon Nowell-Smith. An excerpt from the translation of an essay by Jibanananda Das is reprinted by permission of *The Journal of South Asian Literature*.

In addition, I should like to thank the following for permission to quote from unpublished letters: The British Library (British Museum); Miss Mollie Cohen; O. M. Elmhirst and the Estate of Leonard Elmhirst; J. R. Gould (for A. H. Fox Strangways); The Houghton Library, Harvard University; Humanities Research Center (Academic Center Library), University of Texas at Austin; The Macmillan Company Ltd., London; the Curator of the Rabindra-Sadana (Tagore Archives), Santiniketan, West Bengal; Miss Stella Rhys, Sir John and Michael Rothenstein, Esq.; Mrs. Gillian Wilkinson (for Evelyn Underhill); Senator Michael Yeats (for W. B. Yeats).

I am grateful for permission to use material from the Macmillan Company Records—Rabindranath Tagore Folder, Manuscripts and Archives Division, The New York Public Library, Astor, Lenox and Tilden Foundations.

Transliterations and translations from Bengali, unless otherwise identified, are in all cases my own.

Dr. Edward C. Dimock, Jr., very kindly read the manuscript of this book, and I am most grateful for his suggestions and corrections, as well as for advice and encouragement in connection with this book and also with work undertaken in the past.

The Research Council of the University of Missouri—Columbia has assisted with a grant to cover costs of preparing the manuscript, and Mrs. Cindi Williams typed it with patience and good cheer. I am indebted to Dr. Sujit Mukherjee, who repeatedly expedited the far-flung correspondence connected with this book, and to Dr. M. L. Sharma, an exemplary editor.

Chronology

1861   Rabindranath Tagore born May 7 at Jorasanko, Calcutta; fourteenth child (eighth son) of Debendranath Tagore and Sarada Devi.

1866   Begins learning Bengali alphabet.

1868   Admitted to Oriental Seminary, then to Normal School.

1869   First attempt at versification.

1871   Admitted to Bengal Academy; begins truancy from school.

1872   First acquaintance with rural Bengal.

1873   First visit to Santiniketan; tours North India; spends three months with his father in Himalayas; returns to Bengal Academy, which he leaves at end of year.

1874   Home tutoring until admission to St. Xavier's School.

1875   First public appearance, reciting patriotic poem at Hindu Mela (Fair); first poem published; leaves St. Xavier's School at end of year.

1876   Publishes first literary criticism; first visit to Shelaidaha.

1877   First stage appearance, in comedy based on Molière's *Le Bourgeois Gentilhomme*, by brother Jyotirindranath; contributes poems, including *Bhānusingherpadavali* (Songs of Bhanusingha), to journal *Bhārati,* founded by brother Dwijendranath.

1878   Studies English with brother Satyendranath in Ahmedabad; composes first musical settings for his own poems; goes to England with Satyendranath; attends school at Brighton.

1879   Admitted to University College, London, and studies English literature under Henry Morley; contributes *Iurope Prabāshir Patra* (Letters of a Traveler in Europe) to *Bhārati;* begins first verse drama.

1880   Returns to India (February) without completing studies.

1881   Composes first devotional songs; first musical play, *Valmiki-Pratibhā* (The Genius of Valmiki), in which he has title role; first polemical writing, on England's opium trade in China; first public lecture; sails for England but turns back at Madras.

1882 Publishes *Sandhyā Sangit* (Evening Songs).

1883 Publishes *Prabhāt Sangit* (Morning Songs); marries Mrinalini Devi, of Jessore.

1884 Writes first prose drama, *Nālini*.

1885 Publishes *Rabichchāyā* (Sunlight and Shade), first song collection.

1888 Publishes *Samalochanā* (Discussions), first collection of his essays in literary criticism.

1889 Writes *Rājā o Rāni* (King and Queen), first five-act drama.

1890 Takes charge of Tagore estates in East Bengal; second visit to England (August–November).

1891 First short stories published; launches monthly, *Sādhanā*.

1894 Becomes editor of *Sādhanā*; publishes *Sonār Tori* (The Golden Boat).

1897 Tries in vain to have Bengal Provincial Conference conducted in Bengali; returns to Calcutta.

1898 Becomes editor of *Bhārati*.

1900 Publishes *Kshanikā* (Ephemera).

1901 Revives the monthly, *Bāngadarshan*, which he edits until 1906; moves family from Shelaidaha to Santiniketan and opens school there; publishes *Nāibedya* (Offerings).

1902 Severe financial crisis for the school; death of his wife.

1905 Death of father, Debendranath Tagore; Rabindranath leads public protests against Bengal Partition Order.

1907 Withdraws from active politics and concentrates on educational work; death of son Somendranath; Rabindranath retires to Shelaidaha.

1908 Presidential Address in Bengali sets new precedent at annual Bengal Provincial Conference.

1909 Son Rathindranath returns from agricultural studies at University of Illinois.

1910 Publishes Bengali *Gitānjali*; in London, William Rothenstein initiates organization of India Society, then leaves for India.

1911 Rothenstein visits Calcutta, meets Rabindranath through artist nephews Abanindranath and Gaganendranath.

Chronology

1912   Jubilee observed January 12 by large public reception in Calcutta; departure for England on March 19 postponed by illness; recuperates at Shelaidaha and begins translating selected lyrics into English; sails May 27, with Rathindranath and wife Pratima, reaching England June 2; honored by India Society dinner on July 10; Rothenstein, with A. H. Fox Strangways and T. W. Rolleston, arranges for India Society to publish private edition of translated poems as *Gitanjali: Song-Offerings*, with Introduction by W. B. Yeats. Rabindranath, with Rathi and Pratima, leaves for Illinois October 19; *Gitanjali* published in November; first serial publication of poems in America, in *Poetry* (Chicago); Rothenstein proposes to George Macmillan a trade edition of *Gitanjali*.

1913   Visits and lectures in Chicago, Rochester (New York), Boston; departs for England April 12, for India September 7; Macmillan publishes *Gitanjali* in November; University of Calcutta confers degree of Doctor of Letters at a convocation December 26. Receives the Nobel Prize for Literature.

1914   C. F. Andrews joins Santiniketan staff.

1915   Gandhi arrives from South Africa, goes to Santiniketan; Rabindranath is knighted.

1916   Publishes *Balākā* (A Flight of Cranes).

1917   Traveling via Japan, lectures in United States, but breaks lecture contract because of exhaustion; returns to India via Japan, arriving March 17.

1918   On December 22, lays foundation-stone for Visva-Bharati University at Santiniketan.

1919   Resigns knighthood May 30, to protest Amritsar Massacre; nucleus of Visva-Bharati faculty formed, with opening of Department for Advanced Studies in Indology.

1920   Lectures in England, America, and on Continent to raise funds for Visva-Bharati; American reception disappointing.

1921   Returns to England March 24, has disappointing reception there and goes to Continent to lecture; asks, then rejects, Rothenstein's aid in organizing English advisory committee for Visva-Bharati, thus causing serious break in their friendship.

1922 Initiates Sriniketan, rural reconstruction center, with Leonard Elmhirst as Director; resumes friendship with Rothenstein; lectures in Ceylon.

1924 Visits China, but cancels lectures because of illness; goes to Japan; starts October 18 for Peru with Elmhirst to attend Centenary of Peruvian independence; visit is abandoned when he falls ill in Argentina, where he stays as guest of Victoria Ocampo.

1925 Sails January 4 from Buenos Aires to Genoa; Italian lecture engagements cut short by illness; returns to India.

1926 Leaves May 12 for Italy and is welcomed by Mussolini, whom he meets on May 31 and June 13; goes to Switzerland, where Romain Rolland points out propaganda misuse of Tagore's visit; Tagore issues disclaimer through *Manchester Guardian*; visits England briefly; goes to Continent but gives up visits to Poland and Russia because of illness; returns to India via Egypt.

1927 Tours Southeast Asia (July–October).

1928 Visits Ceylon in May, hoping to continue to England, but abandons plan because of illness.

1929 Goes to Canada, at invitation of Canadian National Council of Education, via China and Japan; plans to lecture in United States universities but is refused entry at Los Angeles because of the loss of his passport; leaves because of discriminatory treatment by United States officials; returns to India via Japan and Southeast Asia.

1930 Begins painting as hobby and pursues it with increasing seriousness; goes to Oxford to deliver Hibbert Lectures, postponed from 1928, published as *The Religion of Man* (1931); has exhibitions of paintings in Germany and England; visits Russia and the Continent (September); leaves October 3 for the United States.

1931 Returns to India via England; *The Golden Book of Tagore* compiled as birthday tribute.

1932 Visits Persia, invited by the Shah; accepts University Chair of Bengali at Calcutta University; publishes *Parisesh* (The End) and *Punascha* (Postscript).

1934 Third visit to Ceylon (May–June).

1938 Publishes *Prāntik* (The Borderland).

Chronology

1940   On August 7, honorary Oxford degree, Doctor of Letters, *in absentia*; publishes *Rogasajyāy* (From the Sickbed) and *Ārogya* (Recovery).

1941   Publishes *Janmadine* (On the Birthday); death on August 7, at Jorasanko, Calcutta.

CHAPTER 1

Tagore's Traditions

RABINDRANATH Tagore was born in 1861, the youngest of fourteen children in a family uniquely gifted and uniquely placed in Bengali society. He lived the first half of his life in times that saw a spectacular accumulation of cultural upheavals and historical crosscurrents; those exerting the most formative influence upon him were the literary traditions of Bengal, which he himself was to affect so decisively, and the inescapable fact of India's subordinate role as a part of the British Empire. To these must be added the characteristic attitudes and activities of the Tagore family, and their role as cultural mediators in situations whose very nature encouraged extremism and violence rather than moderation and eventual accommodation.

I *Bengali Literary Tradition: Prose*

Written Bengali prose, with the standard apparatus of grammars and dictionaries, is a relatively new phenomenon. There is some controversy among scholars about the kind and amount of Bengali prose writing to be dated before 1800, but there is no doubt that the years soon after 1800 were marked by a rapid increase in both the quantity and the quality of prose works written in Bengali and classifiable as imaginative literary writing, as opposed to utilitarian prose such as letters and legal documents.[1] This upsurge of interest in the artistic possibilities of the vernacular was itself due in large part to the fundamentally utilitarian needs of William Carey and the English Baptist missionaries who established themselves in 1801 at Fort William in Calcutta. Making use of resources at hand, they proceeded to train a few picked Bengali assistants as translators of the Bible and other religious teaching materials. This editorial team began at once to devise Bengali grammars and dictionaries, and

21

texts comprising dialogues and compilations of simple stories
and anecdotes of daily life in Bengal. The Carey *Dialogues*
(1801), written, according to their title page, "to facilitate the
acquiring of the Bengalee language" by Europeans, pointed in
an elementary way to the direction to be taken by modern
Bengali prose literature as it rapidly developed during the
nineteenth century. The language of the *Dialogues* was richly
colloquial, and they pictured situations that were pungently
realistic. The possibilities of this partnership between life and
literature appealed at once to the quick imaginations of Carey's
Bengali assistants. For the first time, they realized that their
mother-tongue possessed the resources of an imaginative literary
medium. It was a cultural epiphany that would, with renewed
force, strike succeeding generations of Bengali intellectuals.

Why was this realization so late in coming? It must be borne
in mind that the vernacular had been a Cinderella in the multi-
lingual situation then prevailing in Bengal. Sanskrit was the
language of ancient scholarship and of religious speculation and
devotion; Sanskrit had the prestige accruing from a tradition
in which the religious leaders were also the entrenched cus-
todians of learning, where learning was revered as a divine gift.
The Muslim invasions of India, which were in progress by the
twelfth century, had established Persian as the language of the
royal court and of administration; until 1834 it remained the
language of the law courts. Bengali, overshadowed by these two
prestigious competitors, was relegated to the uses of bazaar
and kitchen. The role of the Prince may be assigned to the
English language, which, fortuitously at first, brought with it into
India literary forms that emphasized, in place of the mystical
and the epic, elements that were realistic, personal, and immediate: the occasional essay and the journalistic essay, the memoir,
the novel, and the short story. These genres, rapidly developing
in the West toward forms now defined as "modern," answered
admirably the needs of a colonial people who wished urgently
to know and understand the outside world as represented by
their European rulers, and wished even more urgently to analyze
the ways in which colonial status was affecting their daily lives.
Their wish to learn English was officially granted in 1835, when
the Government of India approved an English-language cur-

riculum, as opposed to a curriculum based on Oriental learning, for government schools and colleges—institutions founded as training centers for likely young Bengalis recruited to serve the proliferating colonial bureaucracy centered in Calcutta. The supposed advantages of such a curriculum were set forth in Thomas Macaulay's 1835 Minute on Education; it states pontifically that "the dialects commonly spoken among the natives of this part of India contain neither literary nor scientific information, and are, moreover, so poor and rude that, until they are enriched from some other quarter, it will not be easy to translate any valuable work into them."[2]

Macaulay and those who shared his views simply assumed that all of the enrichment would come naturally from the English language and English learning. They failed to foresee that these picked Bengalis, whose acquaintance with English learning, thanks to the missionary teachers and a number of scholarly civil servants, had begun well before 1835, would be so receptive to messages of English individualism and love of social justice. Bengali intellectuals were quick to see that these principles were startlingly applicable to Bengal's subordinate position. "We were dazzled by the glow of unfettered life which fell upon our custom-smothered heart," Tagore would recall in 1917.[3] This heady experience, joined to the dawning realization that the Bengali language was neither so rude nor so poor as Macaulay had pronounced it, gave Bengali prose literature its voice, its form, and its content in a great burst of creative experimentation.

II   *Bengali Literary Tradition: The Lyric*

If Bengali prose was a recent development, Bengali poetry as represented by the lyric was old indeed. Bengali life contains much that can be subtly conducive to an affinity for lyric expression: the folk music of boatmen and fishermen, a natural response to the rhythmic nature of their daily work; the virtuoso character of the classical music, which emphasizes the melodic ingenuity of the solo performer within a strictly regulated rhythmical framework; the prestige given in both court and folk traditions to conspicuous skill in the composition and recitation of poetry; and, reinforcing all of these, the strong individualism of the Bengali temperament. This last, in particular, subtly encouraged what Ernest Rhys, writing about Rabindranath Tagore, called "the lyric impulse which seems so egoistic, but is really so bountiful, pouring out its pleasure for all created things, and transcending the smaller self to attain the greater."[4]

The lyric impulse is nowhere more prolific and pervasive in Bengal than in the Vaishnava tradition, whose poetic conventions Tagore was to adopt and adapt with such skill, to the delight of Bengali readers and to the confusion of many in the West who knew nothing about this very important source and could not decide whether his poems were love lyrics or devotional poems. In brief, Vaishnavism, which is still a potent literary and cultural force in Bengal, was one manifestation of the powerful *bhakti*, or devotional movement that swept through much of India between the twelfth and fourteenth centuries. Vaishnavas worship Vishnu, the Preserver in Hinduism's tripartite concept of the Divine Being. Vaishnava faith and practice have many variations and ramifications, but in general they observe no restrictions based upon caste, class, or sex; they dispense with priests, temples, and other formalities of worship. Central in their group worship are dramatic antiphonal songs of praise, called *kīrtan*. Vaishnava doctrine, which concentrates upon the intensely personal and endlessly puzzling relationship between man and his Creator, is explored and expressed in uncounted numbers of lyric variations upon a single controlling metaphor: the love of Krishna, the eighth incarnation of Vishnu, and Radha, his favorite among the *gopis,* or milkmaids, of holy Vrindavan. The ceaseless cycle of their meetings and separations stands for the relation between God and the human soul.

Orthodox Hindus regard Vaishnavas in much the same way that the English regarded Dissenters and other religious enthusiasts in the eighteenth century. Nevertheless, the motifs of Vaishnava lyrics—aspects of the seasons; the suspense and significance of approaching monsoons; lovers' trysts; the sensual connotations of certain colors, sounds, birds and flowers, times of day and night—recur in the imagery of all of the poetry familiar to Bengalis. From the pampered court poet to the illiterate fisherman casting his nets onto the Ganges, they became highly skilled in the uses of image and metaphor.

To this common heritage of imagery, Vaishnavism added its distinctive religious dimension. "In the Vaishnava anthologies and in *kīrtan*," says Edward C. Dimock, Jr., "the lyrics are arranged to reflect a human love affair against a metaphysical screen."[5] Readers who could not decide between love lyrics and devotional poetry have their answer: like the works of the English Metaphysical Poets, the poems must be read on two levels; to read them literally on one level alone is to lose half of their meaning.

The existence of a common poetic idiom had at least two important consequences for Bengal. In a rigidly structured society, it provided a cultural bond capable of transcending barriers of caste and class, and it assured a ready acceptance for the great works of English literature, when English-language education was introduced in India. If the subject-matter of English literature was new to Bengalis, no one had to persuade them of the power of Milton's epic cadences or the attractions of Wordsworth's nature poems. Thus, during the half-century preceding Tagore's birth, two major literary traditions, half a world apart, were united in a natural partnership that answered both personal and national needs.

III *The Colonial Dimension*

Teachers of English literature in Bengal were delighted by the aptness of their Bengali pupils, but for the most part the teachers underestimated the power of the ideas conveyed by the literature. "Ours was not the aesthetic enjoyment of literary art, but the jubilant welcome by stagnation of a turbulent wave, even though it should stir up to the surface the slime of the bottom," Tagore recalled. Shakespeare, Milton, and Byron were the "literary gods"—as he called them—of his generation, and to these were added the philosophical weight of Bentham, J. S. Mill, and Comte.[6] Although Rabindranath discounted in retrospect the aesthetic aspects of young Bengalis' enjoyment of literature, there was in it a strain of exhilaration at the discovery that they were not alone in their emotional responses to poetry, that these responses linked them to the world beyond India, and that poetry, in that outside world, was frequently in the service of movements for social reform and the enrichment of men's (and women's) lives. At the same time, the increasing refinement of the Bengali vernacular as a prose medium, and the realization that it might be put proudly and not apologetically to literary uses, combined to provide a powerful new means for conveying new ideas to a new reading public that was increasing steadily in literacy and in awareness of Bengal and of India as units in an international whole.

It may be well to survey a few of the landmark dates that supply the historical framework for this emerging sense of personal and national self-awareness. In 1690 Calcutta was founded by an agent of the English East India Company, to become for more than two centuries a principal entry point and control center for British influence in India. In 1757 Clive's victory over the French and the Muslim governor of Bengal, Siraj-ud-Ullah, at Plassey established British hegemony in India. In 1793 was instituted the so-called Permanent Settlement, intended as a means of restructuring hereditary Indian land ownership and property administration, on principles advocated by the British Utilitarian philosophers and economists.[7] In 1833 Parliament stripped the East India Company of its exclusive trading rights, thus setting the stage for a transfer from commercial to legislative control. In 1835 the English system of education was officially introduced, on the lines formulated by Macaulay's Minute on Education. The mutiny of the Sepoy troops in 1857–58 set off a widespread and deeply traumatic rebellion throughout Northern India; this was at once followed in 1858 by the appointment of a Viceroy who replaced the rule of the East India Company and was directly responsible to the British monarch. In 1885 the first Indian National Congress met in Bombay; it was intended as a forum at which Indians from all parts of the subcontinent, which now had English as its educational and administrative *lingua franca*, might meet to discuss common concerns; the Congress rapidly became a forum for the airing of nationalist aspirations. In 1905 Lord Curzon, the Viceroy, ordered the partition of Bengal, ostensibly as a means of increasing administrative efficiency, but in reality a scheme for rendering Bengali nationalists less effective. In 1906 the Muslim League was founded, and in 1909 the Morley-Minto

Reforms granted the Muslims separate electorates. In 1911,
after six years of Bengali protest, at the outset of which Tagore
had been a conspicuous leader, the Government of India annulled
Curzon's Partition order and announced a plan to build a new
administrative city and to move the imperial capital from
Calcutta to New Delhi.[8] In 1912 Rabindranath Tagore visited
England, where the India Society, organized there in 1910 at
the instigation of William Rothenstein, published a small private
edition of *Gitanjali: Song-Offerings*, Tagore's free-verse translations of selections from various volumes of his Bengali lyrics.
In 1913 *Gitanjali* won for Tagore the Nobel Prize for Literature,
the first such award to an Asian.[9]

A pair of scales would serve very well as a symbol to represent
Bengal in the years between 1690 and 1913. The scales would
be more heavily weighted on the side that faces westward.
Indigenous counterweights are added on the opposite side,
slowly at first, then with more speed and assurance as time
passes, but never quite speedily enough to return the scales to
a state of perfect balance. The entire career of Rabindranath
Tagore, who grew up acutely aware of this imbalance, was a
heroic effort, sometimes more, sometimes less successful, to
achieve equilibrium in the combining of Indian values and the
new values imported from the West.

IV   *The Tradition of the Tagores*

Rabindranath's concern for the social and psychological effects
of cultural change and accommodation was acquired at home.
As a child he had continually before him the example of elders
who went out of their way to acquaint themselves with Western
literature, philosophy, history, science, and arts. But whereas
many Bengalis who did this became so enamored of Western
learning that they abandoned all things Indian and slipped their
cultural moorings altogether, the Tagores achieved a certain
balance by going equally out of their way to explore and encourage revival of the neglected arts and literatures of Bengal.
Rabindranath, in his *Reminiscences,* and Krishna Kripalani, in
his biography of Tagore, convey a lively impression of a large
house filled with an extended family group, all engaged in multi-

farious, multicultural activities: Goethe was read in German and
de Maupassant in French, *Sakuntala* in Sanskrit, and *Macbeth*
in English; poetry was written, upon models supplied by Keats,
Shelley, and the Vaishnava lyrics then being compiled and appearing in Bengali periodicals; plays and songs were composed
and performed. There were experiments in the writing of Bengali
novels that drew on Bengali history as Scott had drawn on the
history of England and Scotland; the French short story writers
of the nineteenth century were the models for experiments in
writing short fiction in Bengali. Journals were edited and secret
patriotic societies organized. Friends, associates, and tutors came
and went, all against a background of traditional Bengali life:
the inner rooms were the women's world; the boys were invested
at the proper age with the sacred thread of the Brahmins; the
spiritual life of the household was grounded in the *Upanishads*.[10]

Yet in fundamental ways the Tagores did not fit traditional
patterns. They were Pirili Brahmins, members of a subcaste
disgraced in a past generation, according to the received version,
when a pair of ancestors were tricked into partaking of meat.
Social disapproval eventually forced them to leave their home
in what is now Bangladesh, but they were not passive in temperament; Dwarkanath Tagore, Rabindranath's grandfather, born
in 1794, became a merchant-prince who lived so lavishly that
he was actually known as Prince Dwarkanath. He was a noted
philanthropist and became the first Indian member and patron
of the Asiatic Society of Bengal, founded in 1784 by Sir William
Jones. Dwarkanath further flouted tradition by twice going
abroad, in 1842 and in 1844, at a time when sea voyages were
proscribed for the orthodox. He was received by Queen Victoria
in London and met Max Müller in Paris.[11] He never again saw
India, for he died in London in 1846. There is a deep melancholy
in the thought of this adventuresome man, far ahead of his
time in initiative and in curiosity about the West, dying so far
away from home, where so much that was interesting to a man
in good health must have seemed alien and forbidding in his
last hours.

Dwarkanath left three sons, of whom Rabindranath's father,
Debendranath, born in 1817, was the eldest. Although they were
left affluent by Indian standards, they could not continue

Dwarkanath's standard of living, for one of the consequences of the Permanent Settlement had been to force Bengali entrepreneurs out of business and into land ownership, to the virtual destruction of domestic industry. Debendranath was quite as much of an individualist as his father had been, but the son concentrated his energies upon religion, not commerce. He became known as Maharshi: a man of exceptional wisdom and saintliness. He was a pillar of the Hindu reform group known as the Brahmo Samaj—the Society of God—founded in 1828 by the scholar and social reformer Rammohan Roy. Debendranath devoted his life to study and travel to the holy places of India, and his austerity and long absences from home made him an awesome figure to his children.[12]

The worldly Dwarkanath and the unworldly Debendranath had in common their independence of spirit, which was almost certainly a reaction to the relatively isolated position into which their religious unorthodoxy had forced them. The household, Rabindranath recalled in 1931, had been like "a suburb outside a city. . . . Long before my birth our family had cast off the anchor of society and had reached a distant mooring. . . . That individuality which naturally awoke in the solitude of this family was like the individuality of flora and fauna on an island severed from a continent. That is why our speech had a mannerism which Calcutta people called the speech of the Tagores. It was the same with the dress of our men and women, and with our comings and goings."[13]

These comings and goings could be so largely concentrated upon intellectual and artistic pursuits because, although the princely mode of living had gone forever, the family retained agricultural estates in East Bengal extensive enough to support a relatively leisured urban life style in their Calcutta mansion. It became a center for Bengalis who shared the Tagores' eagerness to find an equitable way of dealing with the flood of Western influences. They sensed that they were living through a classic example of cultural collision, and all about them they observed examples of the extreme reactions to the resulting stress: on the one hand were those who rushed to embrace everything new while abandoning everything Indian; on the other hand were those who went to the opposite extreme of rejecting everything foreign and becoming more orthodox than the orthodox.

Synthesis, a search for a reasonable middle road, was the way adopted by the Tagores and their circle. Both the new and the old must be explored, examined, evaluated by a rigorous standard: did it enhance, or did it detract from the individual's mental, moral, and material well-being? Did it retard or advance the community's sense of itself as a coherent social unit?

In 1908 Rabindranath described both the situation and re-actions to it:

We were, at one time, overwhelmed by the splendour of Europe and accepted its gifts without discrimination, like beggars. That was not the way to make any real gain. Whether it is knowledge or a political right, it must be earned; that is, it can be real for us only if we win it by struggle with obstructing forces. If someone places it in our hands, by way of alms, we shall not be able to keep it in our possession. We insult ourselves by accepting a thing like that and it does more harm than good.

Hence our reaction against the culture of Europe and its ideals. A newborn sense of self-respect has been prompting us more and more to withdraw into ourselves.

This revulsion has been necessary for the purposes of the history which, as I have said, time is evolving in this land of India. The things we had been accepting from the West without question, in sheer poverty of spirit, could never become our own, since we failed to assess their value and used them only as objects for show. As we realised this, it was only natural that we should ask for a change.[14]

He went on to speak of the harmful impasse precipitated by this situation: "The West has come into our homes and we cannot turn it out like an unwelcome guest. Lacking brother-liness, we defeat the purpose of Time. The West, on the other hand, withholds from us the best it can give, with the same consequences."[15]

The Tagores' steady and stubborn advocacy of more and better use of the mother-tongue was typical of their methods for finding ways out of this impasse. Expansion of the bureaucracy and the need for clerks proficient in English had given rise to an in-creasingly prevalent feeling that English was the essential first

step on a precariously balanced ladder that led to the approval
of the rulers, and thus to professional advancement. What had
begun as spontaneous enthusiasm for English literature too
often became examination-oriented rote-learning that fostered
a heartless approach to literature, an unwholesome sycophancy
toward the rulers and a cynical attitude toward the mother-
tongue, and, by subtle extension, toward all that it represents.
The Tagores disapproved of this, and they practised what they
preached. Debendranath's children were thoroughly schooled
in the Bengali language and its literature. When Rabindranath
as a boy read *Macbeth,* he was required also to translate it into
Bengali verse. He and his siblings chafed under this discipline.
Their lessons were suspended only when one of the boys used
grandiose archaic phrases in order to impress Debendranath,
who apparently concluded that this was a bit too much of a
good thing. Their tutor departed with the prophecy that some
day they would learn the value of what he had taught them.
"Indeed," Rabindranath recalled, "I have learnt that value. It
was because we were taught in our own language that our minds
quickened. . . . If the whole mind does not work from the beginning its full powers remain undeveloped to the end. While all
around was the cry for English teaching, my third brother was
brave enough to keep us to our Bengali course. To him in heaven
my grateful reverence."[16]

Such an education is excellent insurance against the risks of
cultural ambivalence. Of all the Tagores, Rabindranath would
stand most in need of such insurance, for he was to have the
most direct and most frequent contacts with foreign cultures.
The Nobel Prize immensely widened his geographical horizons,
and the manner in which this changed his life after 1913 made
him increasingly aware of, and wary about, the delicate balance
between his attachments abroad and his commitments to Bengal
and to India. In 1915, cut off by the war from the possibility
of soon revisiting England, he wrote to William Rothenstein:
"I am like a migratory bird having two homes—and my home on
the other side of the sea is calling me."[17] The migratory bird is
a central metaphor in the devotional songs of the Bāuls, another
of Bengal's *bhakti* sects, whose highly personal character and
metaphysical imagery held a strong attraction for Tagore. His

repeated use of this metaphor of the bird with two nests, one
on each side of the world, was to become a key to his moods,
to the progress of his work, and to the extent to which social
and political pressures threatened to come between him and
his literary vocation.[18]

V Rabindranath Tagore: 1861–1941

Rabindranath, whose name means "Lord of the Sun," was
born on May 6, 1861, in the Tagore mansion at Jorasanko, Calcutta. His formal education began when he was five, with the
learning of the Bengali alphabet. His howls of distress when a
brother and a nephew set off by carriage—the more likely cause
of his disappointment—for the Oriental Seminary in Calcutta
persuaded the family to enter him there at the premature age
of seven. The Seminary's pedagogical methods were Dickensian,
and he was soon transferred to the Normal School, supposedly
a model school on the British pattern, but he recoiled from the
pupils' obscene language and the teachers' insistence that they
sing English songs whose unfamiliar words remained untranslated, and perhaps untranslatable.[19] At the age of eight, he
wrote his first poem; when he was nine, home tutoring was added
to the school regime. At ten, he went to the Bengal Academy,
an Anglo-Indian school with instruction in English. To the
despair of his elders, he promptly began a career of academic
truancy that lasted until 1872, when an epidemic drove the
family to the country; this was the city-bred boy's first close
contact with rural Bengal. In 1873 he went for the first time to
Santiniketan (Abode of Peace), a riverside tract at Bolpur,
some eighty miles from Calcutta, which his father had bought
for use as a religious retreat. Debendranath then took his son
for a tour of Northern India and a three-month stay in the
Himalayas. This, more than the *upanayana*, the sacred thread
ceremony, was a rite of passage, for this was Rabindranath's
first real intimacy with his father. The austerity and dignity
of Debendranath and of the Himalayas combined to make an
overwhelming impression on the boy.

Upon their return, Rabindranath re-entered the Bengal Academy but left it forever at the end of 1873. Thereafter he was

educated exclusively at home by tutors and by his brothers, except for a single year at St. Xavier's School, Calcutta, in 1874-75. Again he declined to distinguish himself; the year is noteworthy instead for several public recitations of his own poems, and for the first signed publication of a poem. Until 1878 these public appearances continued at a rapidly accelerating rate, and he began to publish stories, essays, and dramatic experiments.

The configuration of these childhood experiences is all-important. In even so summary a listing, one sees the shape of his maturity. Here are the thirst for learning and for new experiences and the stubborn rebellion against rigidly institutionalized education. Here also is the influence of his father, brought to bear in a most effective manner at the son's most impressionable age. And here is the deep attachment to rural Bengal and to the mountains as places of retreat from urban life and affairs, combined with the impulse to range over the entire field of belles lettres. With remarkable consistency, all of these comprised the framework of ideas and ideals maintained to the end of his life.

A new phase began, in 1878, with his admission to University College, London. His family had hoped that it might make a barrister of him, but this was yet another abortive academic experience. In 1880 he threw over both University College and the law and returned to India. Again in 1881 he started for England, but this time he turned back at Madras. In Calcutta again, he threw himself into the family intellectual activities, following in particular the lead of his very gifted elder brothers: Jyotirindranath, who was a writer, translator, playwright, and musician, and the scholarly Satyendranath, who had distinguished himself as the first Indian to win appointment to the Indian Civil Service.

Rabindranath married in 1883. After he was father of two children, and after a second, non-academic voyage to England in 1890, his father, in the interests of giving this grown-up son some practical experience, dispatched him to oversee the family's East Bengal estates. Debendranath could not have devised anything better calculated to sharpen the son's literary perceptions and to provide him with subject-matter that he could use to

maximum effect. During most of the 1890's Rabindranath
alternated between a houseboat on the Padma River, and the
family home at Shelaidaha, East Bengal, the estate headquarters.
His sympathetic observation of the Bengali peasant, day after
day through all the seasons of the year, added the element
hitherto largely lacking in his acquaintance with rural Bengal:
real people now moved among the rivers and forests and sand-
banks. These were the Bengali *chotolok*—the "little people" of
the villages and country towns; their songs and stories and daily
struggles to survive became the material of the best of his
stories; they dominate his letters and his journals of the 1890's.
Rabindranath called this "the most productive period of my
literary life, when, owing to great good fortune, I was young
and less known."[20]

A second phase of his maturity commenced in 1898, when
he took his wife and children, now five in number, to Shelaidaha,
where he planned to educate the children himself, in order to
spare them the kind of schooling from which he himself had
so stubbornly fled; he was determined to make learning a
pleasant, natural experience. In 1901 they moved to Santiniketan,
gathered a group of five teachers, and inaugurated what would
now be described as an open-classroom school. Maintaining it
was a perpetual struggle, and his wife sold her jewelry, while
Rabindranath, in addition to being the principal teacher, wrote
ceaselessly—stories, novels, poems, textbooks, essays, a history
of India, treatises on educational theory—and sold the rights to
a collected edition for a mere two thousand rupees.[21]

In 1905 Rabindranath was conspicuous in the anti-Partition
protests; more than a decade before Gandhi appeared on the
scene, Rabindranath advocated nonviolent noncooperation. In
1907, worried by the growing conflicts between Hindus and
Moslems and by the terrorist tactics of the extreme nationalists,
he withdrew, in a protest of his own, and concentrated upon
educational and literary activities. The nationalists could not
forgive his withdrawal; he felt, as he was frequently to feel in
later years, that he gained approval in no quarter except that of
his own principles.

Once again, a family decision—not his father's this time, but
his own—set the stage for a series of interlocking events that

would reshape Rabindranath's life. In 1905 he sent his eldest son Rathindranath to study agriculture at the University of Illinois. Rathi returned in 1909. In the winter of 1910–11 the English painter William Rothenstein arrived in India to observe Indian art on its home ground and to meet Indian artists. Among those whom he met were two of Rabindranath's nephews; through them, briefly and accidentally, he met Rabindranath. In 1912, Rabindranath, with Rathindranath and his wife, set out for Urbana, Illinois, by way of London. Rathindranath intended further study at the University; his father hoped to meet persons interested in his educational theories, and also to find medical aid for a chronic ailment. He carried with him the miscellaneous translations, which he had begun during an illness that delayed his departure for England; the poems had no immediate purpose except whiling away the time of recupera- tion and of travel. Rothenstein was one of the few persons whom he knew in London; the India Society was committed to an annual publication for its members; *Gitanjali* became the 1912 publication.[22] All else followed from that event, and from Rothenstein's immensely wide contacts in England's literary, artistic, and educational circles.

There is a fugal pattern to this first half-century of Rabin- dranath's life. Each new theme is introduced in its turn by an experience of life in a new place: Nature remote and majestic in the Himalayas; the world beyond India, foreign and bewilder- ing to the homesick student in England; Nature intimate and reduced to human dimensions in East Bengal; experiments with natural education at Santiniketan; and, in England again, the start of new and undreamed-of opportunities for finding a middle road between Eastern ways and Western ways. Each of these themes, as it is joined to the others, strengthens and elaborates upon the promise of the opening statement.

In the last thirty years of his life, Rabindranath made nine more foreign tours that took him to Great Britain and Europe, to North and South America, and to the Far and Middle East, as well as three tours of Ceylon. This period has the character of a theme and variations, with passages of drama and grandeur, such as a knighthood received in 1915; his resignation of that honor in 1919, as his protest against the atrocities at Amritsar;

his decision after World War I to change the Santiniketan school
into Visva-Bharati, an international university; his honorary
doctorate from Oxford in 1940. The basic theme, however, was
constant: the search for ways to keep civilization, in the East
and in the West, unified in a world increasingly divisive and
contentious.

CHAPTER 2

Tagore's Lyric Poems

THE lyric, defined as "a brief, subjective poem strongly
marked by imagination, melody, and emotion, and creating
for the reader a single, unified impression,"[1] not only commanded
Tagore's first allegiance, but is also the familiar vehicle of his
introduction to non-Indian readers. During his long lifetime,
he published fifty-four separate collections of Bengali poems;
six more were to be published posthumously. This accounting
includes lyrics that were also songs of his own composition:
Rabindrasangit, Rabindranath's songs, a musical genre unique
in itself and unique in the world. The list does not include his
verse-dramas, which often incorporate lyric poems but lack the
unity of effect required of the lyric poem. It does include what
Bengali writers often call his prose-poems, Bengali free verse
written very late in his career.[2]

These sixty volumes extend the length of the creative gamut,
from youthful experimentation, to mature production, to the
work of old age, retrospective in tone and enhanced by the
effortless practice of techniques perfected over the years. Yet
there are some surprises here, and some departures from the
pattern that one might predict for such a career. The years from
1903 to 1910, which might logically have been a time of maximum
creativity for so prolific a writer of lyrics, saw publication of
only four volumes of poems and songs; one of these was *Sisu*
(The Child), selections from which were to have a great vogue
in English translation but cannot be called work of significant
weight. This was the period of Tagore's participation in the
anti-Partition protests, of his withdrawal from them, and of
his absorption in work for his school at Santiniketan; it was
marked by an immense production of nonfiction and drama, and
it is understandable that lyric output should dwindle in a time
of political upheaval. Yet in the last five years of his life, when

37

he was chronically ill and intensely aware that a worldwide
upheaval was in the making, there came an astonishing burst
of inventive lyric composition: the so-called prose-poems, which
still await definite interpretation and translation.

Of separate volumes of Tagore's poems in English translation,
eleven were published in his lifetime. Of these, only six are
substantial collections that had the advantage of the author's
participation in selection and translation. Of five posthumous
publications, only one is substantial and contains translations
principally by Tagore.

If such an accounting sets forth the imbalance between the
works available in English translation and those still available
only in Bengali, it serves also as a reminder of treasures still
to be explored. An idea of their richness may be conveyed
through explanation of their salient characteristics and of some
effects that were, perforce, omitted in the course of translation.

I *Some General Considerations*

The reader of Tagore's poems, in Bengali or in English,
receives an overwhelming impression of a great variety of
metaphysical overtones. This is true even when the content of
the poems is not explicitly religious. As already noted, the
influence of the *bhakti* movement in India, and of Bengali
Vaishnavism in particular, permeates Bengali culture and was
notably resurgent during Tagore's formative years. It helped
to shape his view of himself and of the world. Being a poet, he
easily and naturally thought, wrote, and spoke metaphorically,
even when he dealt with prosaic subjects. The metaphors that
came naturally to mind were the Vaishnava and related metaphors, in all their variations upon the theme of the intimate
personal relation between God and the human soul. This philosophy of an everlasting search for unity logically attracted a
sensitive young man raised in a family whose members saw the
world as a set of interlocking units and invariably advocated
synthesis as the means of keeping the units from breaking apart.
This view was inclusive: it was not limited to political and social
problems but extended to philosophical consideration of questions of existence itself. "All organic beings live like a flame, a
long way beyond themselves," Rabindranath wrote in 1919.

"They have thus a smaller and a larger body. The former is visible to the eye; it can be touched, captured and bound. The latter is indefinite; it has no fixed boundaries, but is widespread both in space and time."[3] He was referring to the idea of a university, but so unified was his thought on all subjects that one does not violate the original context of his statement by adapting it to his views on man's relationship with God. The vast majority of his poems, and especially of those translated into English, deal, directly or indirectly, with the smaller and larger, or inner and outer, aspects of reality. Nature is the touchstone, again and again, and it is a rare poem by Tagore that does not reflect in some way the skies, rivers, and landscape of Bengal.

In Vaishnava lyrics it is sometimes the human soul and sometimes God—that is, sometimes Radha, and sometimes Krishna—who is the seeker. Radha goes out into the stormy night, wrapped in a blue cloak and with the sounds of her jewelry muffled, to search for Krishna. At other times, Krishna comes to search for her, and she is awakened from sleep only by the sound of his departing footsteps. Now and again they meet, but only briefly; one or the other slips away, their separations symbolizing the fleeting nature of man's glimpses of the nature of God.

Because man is less than omniscient, he is the partner fated to be eternally baffled by the complexities of this partnership. He is the suppliant, and this is the posture that Tagore, in his poems upon this Vaishnava model, assigns to his poetic persona. His supplications are neither abject nor petulant; although they are sometimes outbursts of irritation or frustration, the steady note throughout is a note of loving, wistful longing. These poems are in the mode of Professor Godbole's dance and song that open the third part of E. M. Forster's *A Passage to India*. To the uninitiated Westerner, Godbole appears rather lovable but also slightly silly, and the ceremony seems, in Lionel Trilling's phrase, a "glorification of mess and relaxation."[4] But Godbole's invocatory dance and song are a more colloquial expression of the theme that Tagore affirms with his lines: "I am here to sing thee songs. In this hall of thine I have a corner seat."[5] To the Western eye, accustomed to certain standards of ecclesiastical decorum, Godbole's "braying banging crooning"

accompaniment, his lopsided pince-nez, the jumble of objects
on the altar, and especially the misspelled motto "God si Love,"
speak only of undignified mess and inappropriate relaxation.
But in the contexts attaching to Vaishnava faith and worship,
external mess is irrelevant, and appearances are deceptive.
Behind these is the unyielding tension that characterizes every
relation between man and God. Tagore's poems, of the type best
known to Western readers, are constructed upon a parallel line
of tension (reinforced in the Bengali poems by rhyme and meter
that were unfortunately sacrificed to the English versions)
between the suppliant person's disappointments in the struggle
for union with the Divine Being and his iron-willed dedication
to the search. Readers seeking a parallel among the English
poets may refer to the poems of George Herbert. Tagore's
poetic conceits do not show such careful attention to structural
detail as do Herbert's, but the motif of unremitting search is
at the core of every poem.

This search goes on in the natural, not the supernatural world.
The poems are filled with sounds and suggestions of Nature close
at hand, and this is equally strong in Tagore's less explicitly
metaphysical poems. They suggest daily life lived much out of
doors, and an intimate acquaintance with the cycle of the
seasons. This sense of an ongoing cycle is more imperative in
Tagore's poems than in those of most of the West's recognized
nature poets, for the pattern of Indian seasons is more clear-cut
and the principal annual change, from dry season to monsoon,
is more dramatic than in the temperate zones. Against this
natural setting Tagore designs vignettes and miniature dramas:
a young woman turning her head with a swift backward glance
as she steps into a carriage, a child whose lamp has gone out
on a dark staircase, a newly wedded husband receiving the first
letter from his wife, an empty house, a neglected street. The
details are supplied by indirection and suggestion, and also
present by suggestion is a metaphor of the individual as symbol
for something much larger than himself. Unfortunately, many
readers in the West failed to note these larger connotations and
rested content with whatever they found attractively exotic:
jingling ankle-bells, flower garlands, and incense drifting from
a temple at sundown.

II *Experiments, and Problems of Exchange*

Unfortunately for both the West and for Tagore, many of his readers never knew—still do not know—that so many of his poems were written as words for music, with musical and verbal imagery and rhythms designed to support and enhance each other. The volume *Gitabitān* (Song-Collection) contains words for 2,265 *Rabindrasangit*, in addition to the libretti for several of his dance-dramas or dramatic song-cycles.[6] This is a prodigious achievement (Schubert wrote 614 songs), and the songs are an important demonstration of Tagore's belief in the efficacy of cultural synthesis. He used all the musical materials that came to hand: the classical ragas, the boat songs of Bengal, Vaishnava *kīrtan* and *Bāul* devotional songs, village songs of festival and of mourning, even Western tunes picked up during his travels and subtly adapted to his own uses.

Rabindranath was roundly criticized for including the classical ragas in his experiments. His defense was that music that is not responded to, which does not arouse some answering excitement in the listener, is not fully alive. In 1921 he wrote the essay *"Sonār Kāthi"* (The Golden Wand). The wand of the title belongs to a Prince who will use it to awaken a Princess who has slept for hundreds of years inside a fortified palace. She is surrounded by riches and watched by fierce guards. The Prince represents the living, moving world of the arts—specifically, the new influences from the West. The Princess is the spirit of Indian classical music. The riches that surround her are the great achievements of musical artists through the ages, and the jealous attendants are named "Expertise." They stay awake night and day, so that no one, least of all the Prince with the golden wand of experimentation, may get in and awaken the Princess.

"We can clearly see," Tagore wrote, "that in our country music is not on the move. The experts are saying, music is not a thing that is meant to move, it will stay seated in the drawing-room and all of you must come to it and energetically applaud the performances; but the difficulty is that the age of the drawing-room is gone. Now the place where we stop to rest is the wayside inn. We cannot remain static because we want to pay

respect to that which is static. The river on which we are row-
ing is moving; if the boat does not move, even though it be very
valuable, we shall have to abandon it." Indian music, he believed,
and Indian literature as well, had nothing to fear from the spirit
of exploration and experimentation. The arts of India were not
so frail that the touch of new influences could kill them. Bengalis had already rediscovered the Bāul and Vaishnava songs.
The Prince, in other words, had already evaded the guards. If
the Princess would not awaken, ordinary people would respond
to his invitation and, if forced to choose, would follow him and
leave the Princess sound asleep among her riches.[7]

In Bengali poetry, also, Tagore assumed the role of the Prince.
This was an area in which experimentation was equally unwelcome to the conservative. Serious Bengali poetry in the nineteenth century was still dominated by the rules and aesthetic
of Sanskrit poetics. The Bengali word kabi—poet—and its Sanskrit
root—kavi—meant originally "seer," and in Bengali tradition all
the serious responsibility attaching to preternatural insight at-
taches also to the poet's calling. The Sanskrit rhetoricians and
aestheticians had painstakingly defined and prescribed the successive stages by which a poem leads to an experience of rasa,
a term most simply translated as meaning a state of aesthetic
enjoyment.[8]

Tagore viewed poetry both seriously and reverently, but for
him this did not rule out experimentation. Poetry, like music,
had to be kept in touch with the moving stream of life. He
tried forms and meters new to Bengali poetry. He combined
one of the oldest of Bengali meters, the payār (two lines of fourteen syllables each), with subject-matter drawn from the most
commonplace details of daily living. He substituted the personal,
intimate tone of the lyric for the grandeur and the austerity of
the epic modes. Most important, he initiated a rhetorical revolution in modern Bengali poetry by using language that orthodox
literary pundits considered unsuited to serious poetry: he used
the simpler colloquial diction and verb forms of the vernacular
instead of the highly Sanskritized, more formal and sonorous
diction of literary Bengali. This important change occurred,
appropriately enough, at the turn of the century, marked by
Tagore's volume called Kshanikā. The title refers to matters that

are fleeting, momentary, ephemeral.[9] The impact of these sixty-two poems, written during two summer months, was, however, anything but ephemeral. Bengali critics were shocked and disapproving, and Tagore was reprimanded, then and later, as if he were a cultural renegade. However, he not only made it easier for other Bengali poets to experiment in their own manner, but, at a time when wider international contacts and opportunities were becoming available, he made it possible for them to meet on more equal terms with poets who were leading other national literary traditions away from formality and toward flexibility.

Tagore himself did more than any other Bengali of modern times to widen Bengali writers' international contacts and opportunities. The pivotal event was, of course, his winning the Nobel Prize for Literature in 1913. Inextricably bound up with this great event was the problem of translation, a problem always central to international literary exchange; it becomes especially thorny when, as in the case of Rabindranath's poems, the form is changed from rhymed metrical verse to free verse, when the editors neither know the language of the original poems nor enlist as consultant any one who does, and the general public has neither information about other poetry in the Bengali language nor access to instruction in that language. The curious complex of circumstances and happenstances that brought this about has been documented in detail.[10] What has received less attention is the separation between what Tagore wrote in the first instance, and what eventually became established in the minds of Western readers as Tagore's characteristic poetic idiom. The separation is best explained by a specific example; a similar process of poetic metamorphosis was repeated for all of the poems in all of the major collections published in the West during his lifetime.

The poem that appears as Number 54 in *Fruit-Gathering* (1916) is the Bengali poem, Number 65 in *Gitāli* (Songs; i.e., lyric poems) (1914); it is in a section on worship in *Gitabitān.* If one examines these in reverse order, that is, working from the English version back to the Bengali, one begins to see what elements were lost or sacrificed along the way.

The English version is very slight, and its slightness is part

44 RABINDRANATH TAGORE

of its appeal. The poem sketches the eternal verities in terms
of intangibles, like night, pain, or love, or in terms of the earth,
a material object much too large for the human grasp. Each
idea is neatly contained in a sentence, as if to say that nothing
is too abstract or too large to be outside the province of the
poet.

> The Cloud said to me, "I vanish"; the Night said,
> "I plunge into the fiery dawn."
>> The Pain said, "I remain in deep silence as his
>> footprint."
>> "I die into the fulness," said my life to me.
>> The Earth said, "My lights kiss your thoughts
>> every moment."
>> "The days pass," Love said, "but I wait for you."
>> Death said, "I ply the boat of your life across
>> the sea."[11]

The concrete and the abstract, tangible and intangible
speak to the poet. Each states its unique contribution to his
existence. Each sets limits to its responsibility. The poet whom
they address answers not a word, and this silence implies acceptance of his human condition and his covenant with the
Maker of Life.

What of the same poem in Bengali? Even for readers who
do not know the language, the transliterated text conveys some
idea of the meter and the rhyme:

> *Megh boleche jābo, jābo, rāt boleche jāi,*
> *Sāgar bole, kul mileche, āmi to ār nāi,*
> *Dukkha bole, "Rainu cupe, tāhār pāer chinarupe,"*
> *Āmi bole, "Milāi āmi ār kichu nā cāi."*
> *Bhuban bole, "Tomār tore āche baranmālā,"*
> *Gagana bole, "Tomār tore laksha pradip jālā."*
> *Prem bole je "juge juge tomār lāgi āchi jege,"*
> *Maranh bole, "Āmi tomār jibantori bāi."*[12]

Translated literally, and with no attempt to keep the rhyme
that is readily apparent in the transliteration, the text is this:

The cloud said, "I'll go, I'll go"; the night said, "I go."
The ocean says, "I have reached the shore, I am no more."
Sorrow says, "[I] keep silent, like the mark of His footprint."
The self says, "Merging into that, I want nothing more."

Earth says, "For you is the garland of invocation."
Sky says, "For you, a million lamps are alight."
Love says [that] "age after age I wake for you."
Death says, "I row your boat of life."[13]

Most striking, between the Bengali poem and the English version in *Fruit-Gathering*, is a difference in dramatic situation. In the English poem the self makes no response; in the Bengali poem the self makes a very significant reply: "The self says, 'Merging into that, I want nothing more.'" This is both a reply and a commitment and thus radically alters both the tone and the situation of the poem, which turns upon this fourth line as upon a pivot. Up to this point the attitudes expressed have been negative or noncommittal. The cloud and the night speak of departure; the ocean speaks of self-effacement; Sorrow speaks of silence. But the silent sorrow is also sign and substance of something that endures. As soon as the self states willingness to accept all of these as conditions of life, it becomes the motivator instead of passive subject or recipient. Now earth, sky, love, and death not only recognize the place of the self in the scheme of things but acknowledge it as their own reason for being. Thus the theme of the poem is brought home: by demanding nothing, the self gains everything. Not even Love, which links the self to the cosmos, waits passively; it awakens again and again because of the self's acceptance of all that Sorrow represents. Thus even Death must become the servant of the selfless self.

When the music is added to these Bengali words, the musical imagery states the theme even more explicitly, for the first line becomes a refrain after each stanza, with the additional repetition of the second line in the final refrain. The song thus follows the *aba* form common in Western music. The melody is perfectly intelligible to the Western listener; there is nothing esoteric in its tonality. It is a Romantic song serving as vehicle for a statement about the nature of life and of the universe.

Both the English and the Bengali versions end with the idea
of Death as servant. But the musical imagery does not end there.
It returns by means of the refrain to the first line and its suggestions of departure and conclusion, but the musical line
rounds as if to suggest a circle that is not quite closed. Thus the
song ends on a note that suggests a question asked and an
answer requested. Every line of the song has this inconclusive
rounded shape that parallels the philosophy suggested by the
words: the fundamental questions must be repeated as long as
one lives, and there is no fully satisfying answer to any of the
puzzles of the human condition.

Could Tagore have translated the Bengali more literally? He
could have, and it may be claimed that he should have done so.
All one can say now with certainty is that he chose not to do so,
and that had he elected further to reproduce the rhyme and the
meter in English, he would have confronted an entirely new set
of equally difficult questions.

III   *The Bengali Collections: Before 1910*

Certain volumes and poems are landmarks among the volumes
of Bengali poetry. The first of these to be generally recognized
as a new departure in the tradition was *Sandhyā Sangit* (Evening Songs) (1882). These were the product of a dreary stretch
in the summer of 1881, after Tagore's false start to England. His
brother Jyotirindranath and his wife, Rabindranath's principal
mentors at that time, were away from the city; some members of
the family were plainly disgruntled by his earlier failure to finish
his studies in England; and he settled disconsolately into a
room at the top of the Calcutta house and began to write poems
on a slate, which he found less intimidating than bound manuscript books he had used for earlier work. The result was a series
of poems with titles and, in large part, with content morbidly
and mawkishly Romantic, but notable for their disregard of
traditional metrics. He had discarded the three-beat meter to
which he had become accustomed and had turned to a meter
based on multiples of two beats. "I felt like rising from a dream
of bondage to find myself unshackled," he recalled. "I cut extraordinary capers just to make sure I was free to move."[14] The

collection is cherished today chiefly for Rabindranath's recollections of the historical novelist, Bankimchandra Chatterji, whom
Bengalis like to call the "Walter Scott of Bengal." Rabindranath
arrived at a wedding just as Bankimchandra, also a guest, was
receiving a garland. He placed it around Rabindranath's neck,
saying to the host, " 'The wreath to him, Ramesh; have you not
read his *Evening Songs?*' "[15]

The host had not read *Evening Songs,* and they survive as an
indicative early effort. In *"Āhabānsangit"* (Song of Summons),
the first poem of *Prabhāt Sangit* (Morning Songs) (1883),
Tagore scolded himself vigorously for the twilight vaporings of
the earlier book, and between the two is assuredly the difference
between night and day. *Morning Songs* is all sparkle and sunlight, motion and metamorphosis. The most important metamorphosis is that of the poet himself. In a morning moment of
epiphany he had had a sunburst glimpse of relations between,
on the one hand, the natural world, in its most trivial details,
and, on the other hand, his own potential powers as poet and
his role as observer and interpreter. He never forgot this experience, which he described both in *My Reminiscences* and in
his 1930 Hibbert Lecture at Oxford.[16] His exhilaration was recorded at once in *"Nirjharer Shapnabhāngā"* (The Awakening of
the Waterfall), the most important poem in the group, not only
for its personal connotations, but, as Edward Thompson has
noted, for its use of a river as a central metaphor. In "The
Awakening of the Waterfall" a ray of sunlight enters a frozen
cave and melts the accumulated ice, which grows from separate
drops into a rivulet, and finally into a leaping stream. Thompson calls it a "Himalayan picture," and the description of the
growing river, flowing from the hills through the countryside to
the sea, is a poetic topography of India.[17]

Bhanusingha Thākurer Padavali (Poems of Bhanu Singh)
(1884) belongs with his juvenilia, as these poems first began to
appear in a Calcutta periodical in 1877.[18] They cannot be
compared with *Morning Songs,* published the preceding year,
but they are of interest because they are Rabindranath's early
efforts at imitating the Vaishnava lyrics. He copied their device
of the *bhanitā,* or signature line, a concluding couplet in which
the poet, using his own name, inserts a third-person comment on

the action or theme of the poem. As a gentle hoax, Rabindranath allowed these to be published as by a fifteenth-century (but entirely fictitious) Vaishnava lyricist named Bhanu Singh. (There is a further play on his own name, since *"Bhānu"* is a synonym for *Rabi*, which means "sun.") Rabindranath recalled with glee how a Bengali scholar abroad received a doctorate in Germany for a thesis on this newly rediscovered Vaishnava poet.[19] But Thompson records a conversation in which Tagore speaks with great seriousness about his debt to the Vaishnava poets, and about his good luck in having encountered them at so early an age.[20]

Sonār Tori (The Golden Boat) (1894) belongs to the East Bengal period of Tagore's writings, which saw such steady output of fine short fiction. The poems were written between 1891 and 1893, and they mark the emergence of a concept central to Tagore's personal and poetic life: the *jibandebatā*, or (to borrow Thompson's translation of the term), the Life-Deity. He quotes Prasanta Mahalanobis, who defined it as "the presiding deity of the poet's life—not quite that even—it is the poet himself—the Inner Self of the poet, who is more than his earthly incarnation."[21] This concept, like the memory of the morning vision, became an integral part of Tagore's view of all creative activity. In diction, rhyme scheme, meter, and stanza structure, the title poem, "The Golden Boat," is far simpler than "The Awakening of the Waterfall"; consonantal resonances flow without hindrance from line to line. The poem is allegorical: a farmer whose harvest has been interrupted by the rains sits alone on the riverbank beside his cut grain. A boat arrives and takes his harvest, which has been so plentiful that there is no place for him in the boat, and he is left, beneath the lowering clouds.

There was a spate of critical argument about this allegory, and Tagore had to explain that the boat is the boat of life—the *jibantori*—steered by the Muse and floating on the stream of time, that comes to collect all our works and takes them away to be added to the sum of man's achievements, leaving us behind. Literal explanation of the allegory is heavy-handed beside the rapid flow and the beautiful sound combinations of the Bengali in "The Golden Boat." The important point about the poem is that, like the poems of *Morning Songs*, it was another highly influential experiment in Bengali prosody, and it introduced a metaphor that became a touchstone of Tagore's work: the boat of life, metaphoric ancestor of the *jibantori* rowed by Death in the last line of Number 54 of *Fruit-Gathering*.[22] Unlike *Morning Songs*, *The Golden Boat* moves away from hot-house Romanticism toward the clean, spare lines that came to be called "modern." It is an autumnal collection, in which Tagore, whom Bengalis like to call the "Shelley of Bengal," echoes Shelley's "there is a harmony / In autumn, and a lustre in its sky, / Which thro' the summer is not heard or seen, / As if it could not be, as if it had not been!"[23] In *Niruddesh Jātrā*" (Journey to an Unknown Destination), the last poem of *The Golden Boat*, the cultivator has been taken into the boat. He asks repeatedly where he is going, but the boatman only points toward the horizon.[24]

In the seven years from 1893 through 1900, Tagore produced seven volumes of poems, culminating with the wonderful *Kshanikā* which serves also as introduction to his fully mature work: Thompson rightly calls this book a watershed.[25] Tagore no longer felt obliged to "cut extraordinary capers just to make sure I was free to move."[26] He had discarded the Romantic extravagances of *Morning Songs* and was increasingly comfortable with the informality and succinctness that characterized *The Golden Boat*. In *Kshanikā* he carried these to a new extreme, not only using the simpler colloquial verb forms, but also the *hasanta*, a linguistic device that silences the final vowel of a word and adds greater terseness. This of course played hob with the classical rules for prosody and raised howls of anguish among the pandits: *Kshanikā* began their long feud with Tagore. Thompson relates how a suggested appointment as a Matriculation examiner in Bengali at Calcutta University was protested on the grounds that Tagore wrote bad Bengali; how examination passages from his works were assigned to be rewritten in "chaste" (literary) Bengali; and how the University Senate objected to his receiving an honorary degree, since " 'he was not a Bengali scholar.' "[27] It took the Nobel Prize in 1913 to bring the doctorate in its wake.

The *Kshanikā* poems are secular, personal in the best Romantic manner. Thompson discusses the volume at some length and

gives a fair sampling of its themes.[28] These are set forth with the
wit and wisdom that friends like William Rothenstein valued
so highly in Tagore, the submerging of which in self-conscious
solemnity they so deplored. Each poem creates its own atmosphere by a few quick, concise images; by a surprising use of
rhyme and assonance; and by lines that vary in length and
weight, often bringing the reader up short by means of unexpected variations. Irony is deft and very lightly laid on; amuse-
ment at the small foibles of gentle people is benign and affectionate; there is some delightful fooling of the kind that
Thompson calls "*pandit*-baiting"; love poems strike a note of
wistful rather than wrenching loneliness; and the poet meditates
pensively upon the minor slings and arrows of fortune. *Kshanikā*
is Rabindranath relaxed. The reader of Bengali compares these
poems with the later English prose versions and will not be
comforted.[29]

   Kshanikā was followed by *Naibedya* (Offerings) (1901), one
hundred poems written at the rate of nearly one a day. Where
Kshanikā was lighthearted, *Naibedya* is portentous and somber.
Tagore was deeply disturbed by the Boer War, which he saw
as a sign of worse to come in relations among the Western
powers, with inevitable repercussions upon India. Nor was all
going well within India. Lord Curzon had become Viceroy in
1898, and his zeal for reorganizing the governmental bureaucracy
was well known. This spread alarm and uncertainty among educated Bengalis, who, like most English-educated Indians, looked
to the government for jobs commensurate with their new learning. As the ranks of English-educated Indians grew, competition
for government jobs sharpened. Inflation was on the increase,
and Bengalis began to feel threatened both culturally and eco-
nomically. Resentment and anxiety fostered political radicalism,
just in time for a vehement response to Curzon's publication, in
October 1903, of his plan to partition Bengal.[30] All of this is in
the background of *Naibedya*. It contains poems on religious and
patriotic themes; these find common ground in Rabindranath's
pleas, both implicit and explicit in the poems, for India to hold
fast, no matter what might happen, to dignity, self-respect, and
faith.

IV   *The Bengali Collections: 1910 and After*

The Bengali *Gitānjali* (Song-Offering) is only one of ten volumes of Tagore's Bengali lyrics from which the poems for the English *Gitanjali: Song-Offerings* were selected for translation. Many Bengali critics consider it over-sensuous, so much given to musings and digressions about beauty that it falls short of the standard of his best work.[31] It seems to lack the tension that gives such shape and strength to the best of his lyrics, and to the Vaishnava lyrics. Tagore himself was aware of this. He told Edward Thompson that at the time of writing these poems he was very restless, with many undefined longings to know more about the rest of the world: " 'My restlessness became intolerable. I wrote *Dākghar* [*The Post-Office,* a play] in three or four days. About the same time I wrote *Gitānjali.* . . . I did not intend to publish [the poems]. I knew people would be disappointed, and would say that after *Sonār Tori* they were very poor. But I knew they were very intimately my own.' "[32]

Whatever their limitations, the *Gitānjali* poems are an integral part of Tagore's total poetic canon. Their wistfulness, which, if one were to read all 159 poems at a sitting, would become very wearisome, echoes a dominant mood of *Kshanikā.* The devotional theme in *Gitānjali* is a gentler modulation from the religious strain in *Naibedya,* separated from the contexts of patriotic urgency. In *Gitānjali* both the wistfulness and the devotional attitude are colored by Tagore's restlessness in 1910, in his semi-seclusion at Santiniketan.

The Bengali *Gitānjali* is important for still another reason: it introduced a period of intensive song-writing that is now called Tagore's Gitanjali period, a reference not so much to the Nobel Prize won by the English volume, as to this period of resurgent song-writing. It was as if the malaise that led him abroad in 1912 and the tremendous events that followed also led him back to his particular lyric muse and stirred up a series of fervent responses to her. This had been foreshadowed by an earlier collection, *Kheyā* (The Ferry; or, Crossing) (1906), in which Vaishnava mysticism and metaphors play a dominant but somewhat lugubrious part: Thompson finds this collection of poems "one long wail," and Buddhadeva Bose identifies it with what

he calls Tagore's "dark period."[33] The poems abound with exclamation marks, refrains, static rhyme patterns, and references
to the singer who sits sadly alone. Yet *Kheyā* leads directly, in
both theme and manner, to the poems that frame 1912, the pivotal
year: *Gitānjali*, *Gitimālya* (Song Garland) (1914), and *Gitāli*
(Songs) (1914). These volumes are less self-centered than *Kheyā*
and have more of the detachment of *Kshanikā*, together with its
simplicity. They fairly cry out to be set to music. Nature is
present in nearly every poem of these three volumes, but it is
Nature simplified, needing no exclamation marks to dramatize
the poet-singer's awareness of the scenes that he observes. A
number of the poems in *Gitimālya* were written and dated from
London, Urbana, Gloucestershire, and the S. S. *Lahore*, which
brought Rabindranath home in 1913; they are evidence of his
conscious efforts during his wanderings not to lose sight of his
cultural origins and his Muse.

  Balākā (A Flight of Cranes) (1916) was written between
1914 and 1916, so that it followed immediately upon *Gitimālya*
and *Gitāli*. The poems of *Balākā* reflect a time of account-taking
and of Tagore's reactions to the turbulence of the past four
years: the excitement surrounding the Nobel award and the
knighthood that followed in 1915, the premonitions of political
disaster, and the anxieties of the World War. These did not
render him artistically incapable. On the contrary, they seemed
to galvanize him into new resolutions. "Strangely enough I had
a strong sense of the presence of death this time in the hills,"
he wrote to Rothenstein in June 1914, "which gave me a clearer
perspective of things enabling me to come away with a realisation of freedom I seldom had before. I have a strong hope that
henceforth my works will be truer and my dedication of self
more complete."[34] *Balākā* reflects that new sense of freedom and
that dedication to a new effort at finding his best form of poetic
expression. In the old Bengali fourteen-syllable *payār* and in
radical departures from it, he presents a review and reprise of
motifs and themes that had marked major turnings in his work:
the migratory bird—in this instance, the wild crane; the river life
and the figures in the landscape of riverine Bengal; pilgrims
and other travelers on the open road; human love merging into
divine love; and expectations of eventual union with the Beloved.

The tone of *Balākā* is peaceful, but it is not at all supine, joyful but not raucous. Its tone is set throughout by rhetoric that can only be described as social: the rhetoric of apostrophe. It is as if the poet, who has now seen more of the world outside of India than he has ever seen before, wishes to particularize and personalize his audience, even to compel its attention. This audience is infinitely varied: it comprises the world, youth, the premature spring flowers, a photograph of a long-dead sister-in-law, the wild cranes, even the Taj Mahal, and even Shakespeare. There are no incongruities in this list. Forward motion, symbolized by the flight of the wild cranes, is the essence of Tagore's mood at the time. Everything in the world, the tangible and the intangible, was in a state of flux; the momentum of his identification with this forward motion seemed to sweep him past the old restrictions and the injunctions of pandits and pedants. *Balākā* evidences the sheer delight in experimentation with sounds and rhythms that makes *Kshanikā* a watershed, and the great variety of *Balākā* makes it equally difficult to translate. Kripalani warns everyone, including the author, away from the attempt: "The author's own attempt was suicidal; ours can only be murderous."[35]

The chronology of Tagore's international travels and the record of his extra-poetic activities readily explain why, between 1916 and 1932, no single volume is as adventuresome as *Balākā*. The poet's energies and powers of concentration were too much diverted into other channels, and he was too worried by this diversion to write the kind of poetry that flows from an unencumbered mind. What he had seen of the West during his travels filled him with foreboding, and he poured his energies, as well as his money, into the effort to make Visva-Bharati, his new international university at Santiniketan, an example to the world, of how humanism and humanitarianism might resist and neutralize materialism and worship of the machine. In 1922 he wrote to Rothenstein:

Since science has taken place of religion, Man has been cultivating his faith in the brute and arming himself for the struggle for existence which is the process of the natural selection for the survival of the brute. All the same the fact is that man is man and we must keep him reminding [sic] of it by constantly appealing to his humanity. I have taken that task in my country though the time is unfavourable the minds of the people being overcast with storm clouds of resentment. I have occasional doubts in my mind as to whether I have not strayed away from my own true vocation; if that be so I have come too far off my track to be able to retrace my steps. I must jog on to the end of my days even though I feel weary and homesick for the solitude where my dreams had their early nest.[36]

By 1932, although he had in the intervening years produced a great many poems, he had convinced himself that his career as a poet had ended. He published the set of contemplative poems called *Parisesh* (The End) (1932). But it was not the end. As if to contravene his verdict on himself, he rushed at once into a spate of experimentation. The result was *Punascha* (Postscript) (1932), the first of four volumes in this style.[37] Bengali critics refer to these as prose-poems, and in his preface to *Punascha* Tagore himself speaks of the prose form of the English *Gitanjali* and confesses that he has long wished to experiment in Bengali with this form but had been deterred by timidity.[38] The poems are, however, not prose-poems in the form of the English *Gitanjali*, in which the Bengali lines are cast into solid blocks of prose, or are knocked down into sentences with the self-sufficiency of aphorism rather than the euphonious linkage from line to line found in lyrics that are rhymed and strictly metrical. The poems of *Punascha* are actually free verse, and the lines, if not measured and rhymed, have a poetic progression. The very nature of the Bengali language, with its clear-cut vowel sounds and consonantal verb endings, its repetitive devices for conveying emphasis and onomatopoeia, builds into the poems the assonance, internal rhythm, and liquid sounds that make it easy for free verse to flow musically from one line to the next.

These free-verse or prose poems are lyric in tone, but they are less compact, more leisurely than the early lyrics. This is in part a result of the more diffuse form, but it is related also to their subject-matter. In the affectionate use of such details as endow daily living with both dignity and wonder, and sometimes in elliptical method and compactness, the best poems of *Punascha* recall *Kshanikā*. In the most successful poems of *Punascha,* Tagore is again the observer, but—the reader cannot but be influenced by the knowledge that this is now the elderly Tagore, his international travels all but over, who observes—he is more detached, much less involved in the action or scene of the poem, and content to be so.

One poem that sums up these best qualities and is at the same time deeply moving is *"Ekjan Lok"* (A Man).[39] It is a self-portrait of the poet, lethargic and uncomfortable after an airless, sleepless night, and an account of how the passing of an anonymous up-country man stirs his imagination into functioning once again as a poet's imagination should. The farmer's appearance is quickly sketched in: he is lean, with shaven, shrunken cheeks; he wears patched country-made shoes and a short tunic of printed chintz; he carries a prosaic umbrella on his shoulder and a bamboo stick under his arm. His passing registers on no more than the farthest horizon of the poet's consciousness, and the event, or rather non-event, is described in lazy, loping phrases, like the gait of the tall, lean countryman himself; the very words *"ekjan lok,"* which appear in this part of the poem, have a long-drawn loping quality; it is simply impossible to snap out or to snap off these Bengali words when reading them aloud. But in the next line the poet's imagination leaps into action: he sees himself as he must have appeared to the countryman, that is, on an equally remote verge of the imagination. And then at once we have the countryman suddenly brought into focus. He has at home a cow in its stall, a parrot in a cage, a wife with bangles on her arms—the reader hears the bangles jingle as she grinds wheat for the day's meal. The washerman lives next door, the grocer across the lane, and there is a debt to a moneylender from Afghanistan. In the mind of the countryman, the poet is *"ekjan lok"*—just a man.

A number of equally memorable personalities are sketched in *Punascha* and in the other volumes from this period. Nature, also, acquires personality, even personification. It is less a setting for the poem, as in the early lyrics, than it is a character. One of the best-known poems of *Punascha* is *"Kopāi,"* which is the name of a tiny river near Santiniketan.[40] The poet's mind

idly follows the course of the river, which gradually becomes a
personality contrasted with that of the majestic, all-consuming
Brahmaputra. The Kopai is undistinguished, friendly with its
neighbors, slim and graceful of shape, speaking the language of
those who live along its banks. It is a graceful poem, reflecting
the modest grace of its subject. The serenity of both the river and
the poem reflect the serenity of the poet, a serenity doubly welcome after the confusions and turmoil of his international career.

Tagore's last years saw the publication of poems that are
much more self-centered than those of the *Punascha* group. Even
to the non-reader of Bengali, the mere appearance of the poems
suggests tenseness, for they are tightly drawn up on the page,
and for the most part the poet himself—specifically, the approaching end of his life—is their subject. He was spurred to
composition by illness, or by recovery from illness. In this group
are *Prāntik* (The Borderland) (1938); *Rogashajyāya* (From the
Sickbed) (1940); *Ārogya* (Recovery) (1941); *Janmadine* (On
the Birthday) (1941); and *Sesh Lekhā* (Last Writings) (1941),
published posthumously.

Sisir Kumar Ghose, in *The Later Poems of Tagore,* makes
these poems the occasion for an examination of ambivalences in
Tagore's view of the past, of fame, of his acceptance of life
itself, and of the necessity for leaving it. Lyrical declamations
on the necessity for departing this world were far easier, Ghose
suggests, when the poet was younger and that necessity was not
imminent; in *Prāntik* Tagore renounces desires for worldly
recognition and returns, but very quickly he takes up the idea
that the sense of having lived life to the full is its own reward.[41]
All this, Ghose says, is put in terms of the past and is therefore
in a mode of pathos, and these ambivalences rob the poems of
their effect because the tension is unrelenting, transitions are
lacking, and contact with the reader is soon lost. The poet has
in fact gone out of his way to disassociate himself from contemporary events, a disassociation that in itself represents a
personal crisis for the poet. It represents as well, Ghose says, a
lack of saving cathartic tension in his poems.[42]

It seems unfair to blame a man, at the end of a life of eighty
years, for not being in his last poems what he has never tried to
be. Tagore's actions, his polemical writings, and especially his

letters show that ambivalence had always been a characteristic strain in his temperament. His moods tended to swing like a pendulum, and he often made hasty judgments, as Leonard Elmhirst noted early in his stay at Santiniketan: "Early on, only a day or two after my arrival in November [1921] I had realized that Tagore sometimes made snap judgments on first acquaintance, that his enthusiasm quickly aroused could as quickly evaporate, and that until others, in whom he had confidence, members of his family or staff, had reported back to him of what was afoot, he could be deeply sceptical."[43] Yet these hasty judgments, which sometimes had deplorable results, were related to an important part of his temperamental equipment as a poet: his pervasive curiosity, which even in the last of his poems, never flagged. He had always felt that he must see, feel, and experience, vicariously or directly, as much as possible of the range of human experience. In this he was remarkably consistent. When Mussolini invited him to visit Italy in 1926, then proceeded to make propaganda capital of Tagore's visit, Tagore gave a personal, poetic justification for what was assuredly a blunder in public relations: a poet must know as much as he possibly can about everything, and therefore he had to know about Mussolini.[44] Elmhirst wrote: "Tagore's letter to the *Manchester Guardian* about his visit to Mussolini [repudiating Mussolini's statements about his approval of Italian policies] would have informed all English readers of what had happened but of course Tagore himself was both sad at having been misled in Italy and proud of having at last made his contact with a real Dictator."[45] One appreciates Tagore as a poet who has taken the trouble to display for one's benefit every facet of a lovely gem; one does not complain because looking at all the facets takes up so much of one's time and energy.

V *The English Collections: 1912 and After*

The 1912 and 1913 editions of *Gitanjali: Song-Offerings* were followed by *The Gardener* (1913), *The Crescent Moon* (1913), *Fruit-Gathering* (1916), and the combined *Lover's Gift and Crossing* (1918). No other substantial collection of English translations by Tagore appeared until 1942: *Poems* (all but nine of them his own translations) was published in India, not in England or the United States.

All but one of these translated volumes leave the non-reader of Bengali stranded with respect to chronology and guides to equivalent Bengali poems. The 103 poems of the English *Gitanjali*, for example, comprise fifty-one poems from the Bengali *Gitānjali*, published in 1910, and fifty-two poems from nine other collections whose publication dates range from 1896 to 1914, these last appearing in Bengali after they had been translated for the English book.[46] The poems of the English *Gitanjali* and of the other volumes published in the West were presumably grouped for the effect made by consecutive themes, not in chronological order of composition. Only the 1942 *Poems* provides chronological arrangement and indicates the Bengali source. For the other volumes, there is simply no way to date the translated poems except by tracing them to the Bengali texts, but this is far from easy, even for the non-Bengali scholar with some competence in the language. In most cases the Bengali texts have been so rearranged and condensed that it is difficult to find the Bengali equivalents without searching through the Bengali volumes. One example suffices: the first stanza of Number 59 in *Fruit-Gathering* is as follows:

When the weariness of the road is upon me, and the thirst of the sultry day; when the ghostly hours of the dusk throw their shadows across my life, then I cry not for your voice only, my friend, but for your touch.[47]

The first stanza of the Bengali poem, Number 25 in *Gitāli*, is arranged thus:

> Shudhu tomār bāni noe go
> > he bandhu, he priya,
> Mājhe mājhe prāne tomār
> > poroshkhāni dio.
> Shārā pather klānti āmār
> > shārā diner trishā
> Kamon kore metābo je
> > khuje nā pāi dishā.

> E adhār je purna tomār
>   shei kathā boliyo
> Mājhe mājhe prāne tomār poroshkhāni dio.

Literal translation would be as follows:

> Not your message only
>   O Friend, O Beloved,
> Now and then in [this] life
>   give [me] your touch.
> In all my road-weariness,
>   all the day's thirst,
> How shall I reach the end—
>   searching, I find no way.
> In this deep darkness you
>   speak [to me],
> Now and then in [this] life give me your touch.[48]

When one casts up an account of departures from the Bengali poem, one must note a great deal more than the shifting of the third Bengali line to the position of opening phrase in the prose version. The apostrophe to the Beloved, the cry from the dark that conveys the pathos of the poem, have been diluted. The dark in the Bengali poem is not the dusk of the English version, and shadows are not mentioned: it is *"e purna adhār"*: "this full (i.e., complete) darkness." The idea of the traveler's searching and failing to find the way has been eliminated. The repetition of the second Bengali line, as at the end of the Bengali stanza, has gone altogether. Readers who know only the English prose version are touched by, and respond to, only the atmosphere and the idea conveyed by the prose.

Even when, much later, Tagore came to the translation of his Bengali "prose-poems," he avoided close adherence to details of his Bengali texts. In *"Ekjan Lok,"* which is Number 95 in *Poems,* the first seven lines, translated as literally as possible, are as follows:

> An oldish Hindustani—
>   a lean, long man,
> [With] small moustache, shaven face
>   like withering fruit.

Wearing a short coat of chintz, pleated *dhuti,*
      on his left shoulder an umbrella, in his right
      hand a stick,
Wearing untanned shoes, he walks toward town.

The English version has these lines as follows:

An oldish upcountry man tall and lean,
with shaven shrunken cheeks like wilted fruits,
jogging along the road to the market town
in his patched up pair of country-made shoes
and a short tunic made of printed chintz,
a frayed umbrella tilted over his head,
a bamboo stick under his armpit.[49]

Should it matter to the non-Bengali reader that he has lost the identification of this man as a Hindustani; that the man has a small moustache; that the shoes are of untanned leather but are not specifically described as patched; that the umbrella is not described as being "tilted over his head" and certainly is not frayed; that the umbrella is on his left shoulder, the stick in his right hand, not under his arm; and that his destination is simply "town"?

It does matter: the spareness and economy which are the striking attributes of the later free verse have been rendered altogether too prosaic, impaired by being recast as a solid block of lines made clumsy by gratuitous adjectives. The austerity of the Bengali poem reflects the austerity of the tall, lean upcountry man. The arrangement of the Bengali poem on the page lends a sense of pacing that suggests his steady gait. The distribution of details, dropped neatly one at a time into the Bengali poem, suggests the solid tidiness of his appearance, his probity of character. About him there is nothing superfluous; he turns neither to right nor to left on his way to town. The Bengali poem conveys this impression as the English version cannot.

It is safe to say that there is not one of Tagore's poems translated into English that could not in some respect have been kept closer to the original poem and thus have retained more of the flavor and meaning of the Bengali version. Choices in such matters are the poet's prerogative. Still, in view of Tagore's importance in world literary history, it is also fair to note that the English collections of 1912 to 1918 seem to have been prepared with a peculiar lack of imagination about the range of interest that might be taken or encouraged, both then and in the future, in the sources of these poems which mark so clearly the start of a new era in East-West cultural exchange. Neither the poet nor his publishers could have foreseen the more specific and sophisticated concern with Indian languages and literatures that would characterize both general and scholarly interests after World War II, but there was on the part of both Tagore and the Macmillans a fundamental assumption that the essential East would remain East and the essential West would remain West, to meet occasionally and unilingually at Round Tables where little was accomplished. Such assumptions breed timidity in intercultural relations, and they bred timidity in Tagore when he approached his own translations.

It seems an anomaly that this poet who did so much to mold and direct modern uses of his mother tongue, should have mistrusted it as a reliable basis for closer translation. The anomaly is less puzzling when one examines his correspondence with his publishers and with the friends who advised and assisted them. These letters reveal repeatedly that the source of his uncertainty was not doubts about his command over Bengali, but doubts about his command over English. During the summer of 1913 he veered back and forth between editorial suggestions made by Yeats and those made by Thomas Sturge Moore.[50] In November 1913, after a painful passage during which he accepted, then rejected, Edward Thompson's help in editing his translations, he wrote to Thompson in obvious embarrassment and distress, begging pardon for whatever confusion he had caused, and explaining that the *Gitanjali* poems had such a deeply personal meaning for him that he felt obliged to do any similar translations without assistance. Yeats, he felt, had been right to select for *Gitanjali* only those poems requiring less editorial attention, regardless of their other merits; this approach had the merit, when Tagore worked alone, of helping him to avoid the pitfalls of unfamiliar English usage.[51]

His principal difficulty lay in his failure to follow an inde-

pendent course. When disturbed by criticism of his translated
poems, he would resolve to work strictly alone, taking whatever
praise or blame might come. Yet in only a short time he would
again seek advice and assistance from the West, so that by 1917
Yeats was asking the Macmillans not to ask him to do further
editorial work on Tagore's poems:

William Rothenstein will tell you how much I did for *Gitanjali* and
even his MS. of *The Gardener*. Of course all one wanted to do 'was
to bring out the author's meaning,' but that meant a continual
revision of vocabulary and even more of cadence. Tagore's English
was a foreigner's English and, as he wrote to me, he 'could never
tell the words that had lost their souls or the words that had not
yet got their souls' from the rest. I left out sentence after sentence,
. . . I merely make ordinary press revisions for there is nothing
between that and exhaustive revising of all phrases and rhythms
that 'have lost their soul' or have never had souls. Tagore's English
has grown better, that is to say more simple and more correct,
but it is still often very flat.[52]

Tagore lost the manuscript on which Yeats made his first
revisions, but drafts and letters remaining in various collections
show no evidence that the "revision of vocabulary and even more
of cadence" of which Yeats speaks was done with reference to
the intentions of the Bengali poems. Examination of available
evidence yields an impression of painstaking work done on the
English versions; there is no comparable impression of equal
attention to whether the "continual revision" and deletion of
"sentence after sentence" did violence to the vocabulary and the
cadences of the Bengali texts.[53]

Tagore's correspondence with the London and the New York
Macmillan firms, now in the British Library (London) and the
New York Public Library, confirms repeatedly the fact of his
great uncertainty about his use of English. The most revealing
episode was the controversy throughout 1915 over Robert
Bridges' request for permission to make several "verbal alterations" in the Tagore poems to be included in Bridges' wartime
anthology, *The Spirit of Man*. In long and frustrating exchanges
by Tagore, Bridges, the London Macmillans, and Longman,
publisher of the anthology, Tagore insisted that he did not wish

to offend Yeats, who had first edited these poems. Yeats, when appealed to by Bridges, was not at all offended. Tagore's real reason for his hesitation then emerged: it had nothing to do with Yeats's feelings, but with Tagore's inability to judge Bridges' verbal alterations.[54] This episode was crucial, for it offered an opportunity, never taken up, to reconsider all the accumulated problems of translation and of selection as well, for Western critics had begun to ask whether Tagore wrote on themes other than the mystical and devotional, and whether he could command English of a less Victorian flavor.

VI *The Balance Sheet: The Lyric Poems*

Buddhadeva Bose, opening a series of lectures on Tagore at Bombay University, remarked on the difficulty, for a Bengali poet of the post-Tagore generation, of commenting dispassionately on Rabindranath. "One can be *too* familiar with a poet's works," he said, "and altogether too involved and indebted, to be able to find the right words for one's feelings about him, or even to be sure what those feelings are. And this is the position in which I find myself in relation to Rabindranath Tagore."[55] He went on to note that a supposedly *avant-garde* Bengali journal had recently deplored his "blind devotion" to Tagore, while others attacked him for a want of reverence for his great predecessor.[56]

His dilemma is typical of the position of all modern Bengali poets. Tagore's influence has been so pervasive, his personality so impressive, his accomplishments so varied, that it is very difficult to break away, to do something—anything—that may be recognized as a new departure in Bengali poetry. Those who decry his influence most vociferously, feeling it as a dead weight on Bengali letters and criticism, cannot help but pay him the indirect compliment of their rebellion. Buddhadeva Bose opens a valuable and subjective survey of Bengali poetry and prose with a chapter titled "Rabindranath"; its first sentence is this: "Rabindranath Tagore is a phenomenon." Buddhadeva describes him as "a force like Nature's, expressing itself in literature." He goes on to say that although Tagore is not, in his opinion, to be classed with Shakespeare or Yeats, his "unique merit is his

quantity, his immense range, his fabulous variety.... Rabindranath is the world's most complete writer."[57]

In a subsequent chapter on Bengali poetry, Buddhadeva
specifies that he will include Rabindranath, but "it is not to my
purpose to bring him in unless unavoidable."[58] And bringing
him in, directly or indirectly, positively or negatively, is manifestly unavoidable. Kalidasa is referred to as a touchstone for
the ancients, Tagore for the moderns. Bengali poets of the mid-
twentieth century are on the horns of a dilemma, for it is equally
impossible to imitate Rabindranath and not to imitate him. The
poet Satyendranath Datta, who died in 1922, had received a kind
of critical appreciation that was denied Tagore: Datta was a
"Rabindranath Made Easy . . . in verse."[59] The pictorial quality of
the poems of Jibanananda Das, who died in 1954, attracted the
special attention of Tagore. Amiya Chakravarty is, next to
Tagore, the most widely traveled of modern Bengali poets and
critics.[60] Samar Sen is "our only poet who has written only
prose poems and no verse at all"—that very prose-poem form
established in Bengali by Rabindranath's *Punascha*.[61] Bishnu
Dey has a bad habit of "slicing out lines from Rabindranath,
changing them slightly and whimsically, and placing them in
incongruous contexts."[62] On the other hand, Sudhindranath Datta,
whose work is unique because his love poems shy away from
the mystical love of the Vaishnavas and the idyllic love found
in Rabindranath's *Kshanikā* poems, "gleans freely from Tagorean
harvests . . . in a straightforward manner, never trying to conceal what is true for him and each of his contemporaries."[63]

And so it goes. Tagore himself could not avoid his own
ubiquitousness. Buddhadeva Bose quotes from a letter in which
Tagore confesses that he is partial to Sudhindranath Datta's
poetry because it has " 'taken much of its shape, and that quite
unhesitantly, from my work.' "[64] This is less immodesty than
recognition of a fact—and of a common problem.

The common problem arises not only from Tagore's range
of achievement, but also the eighty-year span of his lifetime.
At least three generations of Bengali poets were born during
his working years, which continued almost literally to the day
of his death. Distancing themselves from him chronologically,
as well as in a literary sense, was manifestly impossible. "I am

afraid," said Buddhadeva Bose, "we cannot help taking him for granted, and this is what a critic should never do."[65]

Western readers and critics, on the other hand, had problems of the opposite sort. Although since 1800 many hundreds of British civil servants had used Carey's *Dialogues* and dictionaries and the succeeding texts to learn a utilitarian Bengali for their work in India, Bengali literature was an unknown quantity in England. James Drummond Anderson, retired Indian Civil Service official who in 1912 was Lecturer in Bengali at Cambridge, told Rothenstein that "only yesterday I met a lady who had travelled widely if not wisely in India and had never heard that there was any modern literature in India at all."[66] Bengalis studying in England were, for the most part, more eager to display knowledge of English literature than to proselytize on behalf of their own. If this was the state of affairs in England, which for more than a century had ruled India out of Calcutta, how much more true was it of the United States?

What both countries could and did take for granted was the facile stereotype of the Indian as mystic and guru. Tagore's initial appeal in the West was to those whose own interests tended in that direction. Friends like Rothenstein, in whose makeup tentative mystical leanings were combined with a sturdy pragmatism, saw in Tagore much that they found lacking in Western culture. In the summer of 1912 Rothenstein wrote to urge George Bernard Shaw to come and meet Tagore:

I want you to meet Rabindra Nath Tagore, for you have not met many saints in your life, and perhaps as few poets. He too must see—is seeing clearly—that England is not Anglo-India, and you must come up to talk with him. He represents all that is religious, literary, democratic, scholarly and aristocratic in Bengal, and if there were no other representative we should look upon India as the most perfect country in the world. This sounds like too youthful enthusiasm—but our gifts lie in power and tact and vitality rather than in personal perfection, and you will each give the other an insight into qualities suspected but not actually experienced perhaps. Will you and Mrs Shaw come up to lunch—our friend is a vegetarian of course, and there is a trivial but additional reason for paying him homage. Of course you ought both to come to the [India Society] dinner—we only welcome Maharajas in this country, at best politicians, and here we have a real seer among us, and what is decent among us should do him and his country all possible honour, but I fear you are hopeless regarding things of that kind.[67]

Rothenstein, all unconsciously, sums up emphases that were to become attached to Tagore in his future relations with the West: he was to be regarded as a compendium of all the civic and cultural virtues, an unofficial ambassador, and an embodiment of a kind of mystical perfection rendered impossible by the Western pursuit of material things. Above all, he was to be regarded as saint and as seer. This placed a very great burden on his fragile poems, the only medium through which most Westerners would know him.

Yeats's famous Introduction to the English *Gitanjali* sounded the keynote for what seemed, from such descriptions, tantamount to a Second Coming. When his Introduction is detached from the totality of Yeats's work and reputation, it cannot be faulted for sincerity and genuine enthusiasm, but it must be assigned to the breathless school of criticism. Comparison with the equally simplified Introduction by Edward C. Dimock, Jr., to *In Praise of Krishna* reveals the shallowness of Yeats's (and nearly everyone else's) scholarship on the subject in 1912. As Yeats confesses freely, such information as he had came at second hand from literary amateurs: from Dr. D. N. Maitra, the "distinguished Bengali doctor of medicine," who happened to be traveling westward with Tagore's party, and from other Indians who had turned up from time to time—in particular, the theosophical Mohini Chatterjee who had visited Dublin in 1885.[68] The qualities of *Gitanjali* and of Tagore himself that Yeats found most attractive were innocence, simplicity, spontaneity, and the sense of a mythic tradition, dim, undefined, but certainly reaching back to the unrecorded past: all these were attributes that Yeats was determined to reconstruct for Irish literature. He would have been the first to cry horror at the thought of his having given aid and comfort to England's imperial views, yet a politically useful stereotype obtrudes between the lines of his Introduction. Tagore is not an ascetic, but he is nevertheless a "saint." The West lacks the "reverence" for its great men that Bengalis seem to have for Tagore. His father had sat

immovable in meditation for two hours daily; his philosopher
brother Dwijendranath was a kind of St. Francis on whom the
birds and the squirrels alighted without fear. Both Tagore and
Indian civilization are "content to discover the soul and sur-
render [themselves] to its spontaneity."[69] Serenity and content-
ment were what England most coveted for India, whether it
was to be found in the soul or elsewhere: Bengalis who sat
immovable were less likely to stir up political discontent of the
kind that had made the years of anti-Partition protest so
turbulent.

Several themes from Yeats's Introduction were seized upon,
not always accurately, by reviewers. His carefully remembered
quotation from Dr. Maitra's explanation of Tagore's position in
India was adopted and repeated, with variations, but without
its accompanying qualification. *The Athenaeum*, whether through
a misreading of Yeats's Introduction or of India's demography,
took this to mean that Tagore's name was "known through the
length and breadth of India," thus omitting Dr. Maitra's explanation that Tagore's name was known in 1912 *wherever Bengali
was spoken* in India.[70] As Bengali was spoken outside the north-
eastern part of the subcontinent only by the scattered groups
of Bengalis who had migrated to other provinces, this left the
vast majority of Indians unaware of both Tagore and his poems.
It was only through the English translation, and the spate of
translations into other Indian languages that came after the
Nobel Prize, that Tagore's name became really well known
"throughout the length and breadth of India." *The Spectator*
was similarly imprecise; it stated that Tagore's work, "Mr. Yeats
tells us, is widely read and reverenced among his countrymen."[71]
The average reader in the West was not likely to pause and
consider that in that context "countrymen" referred in fact
principally to Bengalis. This impression of Tagore as an all-India
literary star was passed from reviewer to reviewer and helped
to cloud the West's initial conception of Tagore's position in his
own country. Equally absent from Yeats's Introduction and the
reviews were the highly pertinent facts of the criticisms of
Tagore by the Bengali literary Establishment and, further, the
fact that as a member of a family at the center of the Brahmo

movement, Tagore's philosophy and works were anathema to orthodox Hindus.[72]

A theme repeated frequently by reviewers was that of the contrast between Tagore's Eastern philosophy and outlook, to which was attached the catch-all label of "mysticism," and the West's failure to achieve a comparable tranquility. Readers were told, in fact, that they could not hope to do so. This syndrome—the colonizers' self-denigrating comparison with the spiritual resources of the colonized—is a familiar one in Western writing about the East. It does little to elucidate Eastern writing for willing but uninitiated Western readers. It was present in full measure in reviews of *Gitanjali*, along with copious allusions to Western poets who fell short of the mark set by Tagore. *The Times Literary Supplement* reviewed the book soberly and favorably, bracketing *Gitanjali* with the Psalms of David and the poems of George Herbert. The note of self-denigration appeared in the conclusion: "Some perhaps will refuse to fall under the spell of this Indian poet because his philosophy is not theirs. If it seems to us fantastic and alien, before we despise it, we should ask ourselves the question, What is our philosophy? We are very restless in thought, but we have none that poets can express. For it is either pure theory or of the nature of scientific experiment. At best it is applied coldly to life rather than drawn out of life with the warmth of experience still in it."[73]

In a review of the India Society edition, the *Athenaeum* reviewer found the translations "of trance-like beauty; their negation of movement and colour, and the deliberate flavorlessness of their simplicity are appropriate to the vein of essentially Oriental mysticism which supplies throughout the poet's inspiration."[74] This reviewer found Yeats's Introduction "somewhat impetuous" but immediately outdid him in impetuousness by saying that beside Tagore's poems the accents of Blake were those of an "ungoverned child."[75] In a notice of the Macmillan edition, the *Athenaeum* reviewer stated that Tagore's verse "has a serenity which is one of the lessons most needed by the restless peoples of the West."[76] This talk of trances, negation, and deliberate flavorlessness was scarcely conducive to rigorous study of the poems themselves.

In general, American reviewers followed the lead of the English commentators, making the same points and stressing the same themes.[77] Several of the most influential articles, in both countries, were written by friends who, like Yeats, had met Tagore through Rothenstein. Their writing reflects the strong impression that Tagore had made upon them, although they were sometimes moved by their enthusiasm to overdo the saintliness theme and to perpetuate the generalizations about the extent of his fame in India. Evelyn Underhill, who wrote the review for the London *Nation*, brought to her study of *Gitanjali* not only her considerable knowledge of the literature of mysticism, but also her respect for Tagore. During the summer of 1913, she revised Tagore's translations of poems by the fifteenth-century Benares mystic Kabir, for which she was also to write an Introduction. To Tagore she wrote:

I want so much to tell you—but it is not possible—what your kindness and friendship has meant to me this summer, and will always mean to me now. This is the first time I have had the privilege of being with one who is a Master in the things I care so much about but know so little of as yet; and I understand now something of what your writers mean when they insist on the necessity and value of the personal teacher and the fact that he gives something which the learner cannot get in any other way. It has been like hearing the language of which I barely know the alphabet, spoken perfectly.[78]

Her review of *Gitanjali* is as straightforward as her letter. She does not gush, does not patronize the general reader, and does not accuse him of spiritual incompetence. In rococo contrast to the Underhill review is that by the novelist May Sinclair, for *The North American Review*. She compares the *Gitanjali* poems at once to the Psalms of David, and explains that she first heard Tagore's poems when "Mr. Yeats turned Mr. Rothenstein's drawing-room into a holy temple by reading a dozen or more of them to about a dozen people." A friend had later asked her to explain the poems, but "deep seated in his mind was the conviction that devotional poetry is not and cannot be pure poetry"; the friend's taste for and understanding of devotional poetry

was confined to the level of "Lead, Kindly Light," and Miss Sinclair abandoned the effort to explicate Tagore's poems, which
have "a music and rhythm almost inconceivable to Western ears."
This theme, certain to alienate all who cared for "Lead, Kindly
Light," is stressed repeatedly: "To the Western mind there is a
gulf fixed between the common human heart and Transcendant
Being." Having told Western readers that they cannot hope to
understand Eastern writing, Miss Sinclair then instructed them to
do so forthwith: "But as the East is subtler than the West, and as
of all Eastern races the Bengali is the subtlest, so an extreme subtlety of feeling and of rhythm is the first quality that strikes you in
the songs of this Bengali poet." They have "strange music [that is]
lost to us, . . ." Miss Sinclair has already marshalled a remarkable
array of Western poets, all of whom fall short of the standard
set by Tagore: Swinburne, Milton, Wordsworth, Shelley,
Crashaw, Francis Thompson, Henry Vaughan, and "Blake at
his simplest": "not even Dante and St. John of the Cross, though
they stand nearest (they are very near) to this great mystic poet
of Bengal." She calls the roll of Western mystics: "No. There
is nothing in the Western world to compare with these poems
but the writings of those mystics who were also saints: St. Augus-
tine, St. Thomas à Kempis, St. Francis of Assissi, St. Julian of
Norwich, St. Catherine of Genoa, St. Teresa; and, above all,
St. John of the Cross in 'the Dark Night of the Soul.'" She
concludes with a reference to Tagore as a Walt Whitman,
"(that robust and boisterous Vaishnavist of the Western West)
without his boisterousness."[79]

Reviews of this kind not only did not help Tagore but actually
harmed both him and the cause of international literary exchange.
They gave less friendly commentators grounds for jibes of the
sort that appeared in the New York Nation; it cited Miss Sinclair's review as evidence of the "gilded Grub Street of present-
day London, with its opulent Socialists and intellectual mounte-
banks and loose-living saviours of society and propounders of
radical-tory paradoxes and Celtic moon-dreamers and hysterical
feminists." It gave no credence whatever to May Sinclair's
"sibylline utterances," and advised readers that if they could
"forget the thaumaturgic Mr. Yeats turning Mr. Rothenstein's
drawing-room into a holy temple, forget that this is the supreme

event of literature," they would then enjoy *Gitanjali* as a flower from the autumn of romance.[80]

Walt Whitman was a special interest of T. W. Rolleston, who as Treasurer of the India Society had seen a good deal of Tagore in London. However, Rolleston, in a review of *Gitanjali* for *The Hibbert Journal* kept Tagore and Whitman in more balanced perspective. "After Walt Whitman and Nietzsche," he wrote, "it is useless to ask [the younger generations] to listen to any philosophy which denies life. Not even the East will do so now."[81] "It would not be surprising," he wrote, "if this book became a landmark in our literature, because it is one of the first and the finest expressions of a pure religious fervor which has not needed for its passion and its inspiration the attachment to some intermediate object, some physical incarnation of deity, some human or semi-human personality, some definite historical or national channel of access to the divine."[82] This statement may be somewhat too sweeping, but Rolleston, like Evelyn Underhill, wrote in a straightforward manner, avoiding denigration of Western capacity for spiritual development.

By far the most scholarly and most important of all the reviews was that in *The Fortnightly Review* by Ezra Pound, who in 1912 was acting as a kind of resident editor and secretary to Yeats. This brought Pound, along with Yeats, into the circle of Rothenstein's friends introduced to Tagore, and his article was written one month after Pound had met Tagore in Yeats's rooms in London. Although Pound quickly became impatient when Tagore's translated poems adhered too long to the model set by *Gitanjali*, his first enthusiasm resulted in Tagore's first American periodical publication, in *Poetry*, edited in Chicago by Harriet Monroe.[83] Other reviewers had noted the fact, conveyed to them by Bengali acquaintances, that Tagore's poems were also the words to songs, but Pound, from his knowledge of medieval French song tradition, put this into a context more meaningful to Western scholars. "The appearance of 'The Poems of Rabindranath Tagore' is, to my mind, very important," he wrote. "I am by no means sure that I can convince the reader of this importance.... He must read it quietly. He would do well to read it aloud, for this apparently simple English translation has been made by a great musician, by a great artist who is familiar with

a music subtler than our own." This was not a facile East-West
comparison; it is based on fact. Indian music *is* more subtle than
Western music; its semi-tones and intricate chromatic progres-
sions require greater subtlety on the part of the unaccustomed
Western ear. Indian musical tradition is far older than any in
the West, and Pound tried to put this into perspective for Western readers by explaining that although Bengal might appear
modernized on the surface, its arts are grounded in a heritage
similar to that of twelfth-century Provence. Tagore's songs
struck Pound as falling somewhere between Provençal canzoni
and roundels and the "odes" of the *Pléiade.* Tagore, being unencumbered with rules of harmony, was free to draw from many
sources, particularly the *ragini* (variations on the *raga,* or basic
melody) of Indian classical music, which contribute to poetic
uses very specific sensual associations with seasons of the year
and hours of day and night.

Unfortunately, Pound fell into extravagance with his often-
quoted statement that "when I leave Mr. Tagore I feel exactly
as if I were a barbarian clothed in skins, and carrying a stone
warclub, the kind, that is, where a stone is bound into a crotched
stick with thongs." Here he made an East-West generalization,
redeemed partially by his eloquence: the *Gitanjali* poems have
"a sort of ultimate common sense, a reminder of one thing and
of forty things of which we are over likely to lose sight in the
confusion of our Western life, in the racket of our cities, in the
jabber of manufactured literature, in the vortex of advertise-
ment." Less redeemable is his observation that Tagore "has well
served [India's] Foreign Office" by giving the West beauty "that
is distinctly Oriental . . ."[84] As India was even then becoming increasingly aware that she *had* no Foreign Office of her own, and
as Tagore, with reason, was becoming hypersensitive about
political strings being attached to his poems, this remark was
extremely tactless—but it was less political tactlessness of the
kind in which Pound was later to indulge, than it was a typically
thoughtless Western remark about the East, made with intentions
of paying a sincere compliment.[85]

The article by Ernest Rhys in *Nineteenth Century and After*
is not as incisive as Pound's, but it is significant because Rhys,
a few months later, began to write what would be the first

book-length study of Tagore by any of the Englishmen who
had known him at the time of his introduction to the West.
It is worth while, therefore, to examine briefly the genesis and
reception of this book.

Rhys, a Welsh poet and essayist, was a gentle, independent
man, unworldly, his daughter recalls, in a way that resulted in
a quite practical and very effective stubbornness concerning things
about which he cared deeply.[86] His diligent, dedicated caring
about books brought about the landmark Everyman's Library
of J. M. Dent, which Rhys originated and edited. He cared also
about Wales and his Celtic heritage, and Tagore's poems struck
sympatheic chords. Rhys, like Yeats, had first heard about them
from a chance Bengali acquaintance in London, "in a way indeed
to make one's ears tingle."[87] His imagination was particularly
stirred by the knowledge that in Bengali the poems were words
for songs as well. His review of *Gitanjali* indulges a bit in hyper-
bole at its conclusion, but for the most part it concentrates on
advising Western readers how to get the most out of these Indian
poems—and he does not discourage them by telling them at the
outset that understanding them is impossible. It is useful to keep
in mind, he says, "that the title does not mean songs in the
conventional sense with which we use the term, but songs really
to be sung.... The whole spirit of the book is musical, and if
the emotion at times seems to be affected by the Indian tradition
and a note of Quietism, and the rapture is held in suspense, the
songs, even in the English prose-rhythms are irresistibly impulsive." The lyric tradition had been submerged or lost in
England: modern poets no longer write to musical or any other
accompaniment except "that of the literary make-believe."
Tagore had surmounted this difficulty, "and the gain to his
poetry has impressed even Mr. W. B. Yeats, whom I can remember speaking two or three years ago with a fine contempt of
those who tried to relate verse to music."[88]

Rhys's empathy with Tagore proved to be more durable than
that of either Yeats or Pound. After Tagore had returned to
India, Rhys wrote:

What are leagues of sea between true friends? Alas, I am afraid
they are something that can hinder our heavier thoughts from

flying. But I would like you to realise how much you meant to us
while you were here,—and still how much you count now you are
gone again. You have indeed made a difference in our lives,—the
very room that knew you is not as it was. For myself, you have
quickened my whole feeling for the sun, the light,—all those things
that reveal the spirit, and remake the vision of the world; and you
have brought back the old fond belief of my youth in the ideal
Life that is behind the real.

It is good for me now to think of that Beatitude, because events
are driving me every day so fast out of the true centre. Publishers'
quarrels, the mania for books, the call for rapid restless activity,—
they all tend to break up the peace of one's mind; and you cannot
tell how much I am inclined to envy you your Indian quiet at
times. Remember us, I pray, in our London whirlpool.[89]

Late in 1913, Rhys concluded a long letter as follows:

I am tempted now to add a mention of a desire that has crossed
my mind latterly at odd moments,—a desire to attempt a book
about you, my dear friend and master, and about your books and
ideas, your life and Indian circumstance. It is a drawback, I know,
that I have never been in India: still, that might be got over
perhaps. Let me know what you think about such a project.[90]

Tagore's letters to Rhys have not survived, and it is not certain
whether he responded at once to Rhys's proposal. In January
1914 Rhys wrote: "It would give me much gratification to be
able now to write out, at greater length, my own appreciation
of your ideas and your intrinsic philosophy. I had almost made
up my mind the other day to ask Macmillan & Co. to consider
such a book; but they have an old feud with my publishers,
Dent & Co., which might affect their feeling about such a proposal? Again, comes the question whether I know enough about
India, and the Bengal tongue and spirit of life, to write intelli-
gently about your work?"[91]

In February he told Tagore, "You know how glad I should
be, to widen your orbit here, and so doing to bring India nearer
to our mental coasts and human regions?"[92]

Tagore presumably responded favorably, for by May Rhys
was beginning his research. He had turned to Rothenstein, as

the mutual friend who had observed Tagore in his Calcutta home; Rhys told Rothenstein: "I have, unwisely perhaps, undertaken to write an account of Tagore and his poems, and need all the help that can be got from first-hand sources."[93] To Tagore he wrote: "My one real task here [during a holiday on Exmoor] is to write the book on 'Gitanjali' and your other writings, with some account of their writer. But I find myself wofully deficient, when trying to re-create a sort of apparency of Bengal, and a vision of your self in this moorland solitude [i.e. Exmoor] . . ."[94]

Rothenstein's letters to Rhys also are lost, but his response was encouraging, and Rhys replied: "Chunder [Dinesh Chandra] Sen's big book on Bengali poetry has given me a new idea of R. T.'s antecedents—some of his forerunners are curiously like him. My task is to get at the reality, and not to minister to any cult: but it is, as you surmise, hard for an outsider to penetrate the Indian confines, and get home there."[95] Late in June, Rhys was writing to Tagore from the Rothensteins' farm at Far Oakridge: "You will recognise this Gloucestershire heading. . . . We have indeed been very Indian in our [word illegible] and topics. —I find W. R. a wise spectator and discourser of our great world, and its powers and cares and the rest,—and his understanding of your part in it is real and simple-subtle."[96]

Ernest Rhys's book, *Rabindranath Tagore: A Biographical Study*, published after all by Macmillan, appeared in 1915 in both England and the United States. It was unfortunate that another book, *Rabindranath Tagore: The Man and His Poetry*, by Basanta Koomar Roy, a Chicago-based Indian, appeared at the same time. Particularly in the United States, the two books were reviewed together in a number of influential papers and periodicals, with Rhys's book usually pronounced superior in style and Roy's being given the greater share of space, as well as being rated more complete as a biography. The reviews contain a full quota of careless generalizations about Tagore's fame in India, about his Bengali background being full of mystery (and therefore inaccessible to the Western reader), and about the parallels with Western poets and mystics.[97]

Throughout these reviews run two disturbing undercurrents. One is an assumption, on both sides of the Atlantic, that anything any Bengali said about Tagore was more authoritative than anything any Westerner could say about him. This tells more about the reviewers' attitudes toward India than about the books under review; it is first cousin to the insulting cliché to the effect that "all Orientals look alike," for it assumes a seamless uniformity in Bengalis' knowledge and opinion of Tagore. About Roy himself, little is known. He was born in Orissa, came to the United States about 1910, studied at the University of Wisconsin, and, like a number of other expatriate Indians, had a vague career thereafter as extension lecturer and journalist. In January 1913 he visited Tagore in Urbana, and he is blatantly self-serving in his account, for which there is no authority other than his own, of a conversation with Tagore in which Roy claims to have planted in Tagore's mind the idea of the Nobel Prize, and to have spurred the poet on to additional translations that eventually made the Prize a reality.[98] This is contradicted by all the documentary evidence of Tagore's voluminous personal and business correspondence with Rothenstein, Yeats, Thomas Sturge Moore, A. H. Fox Strangways, and the London Macmillans, all of whom were already engaged in preparing his next volumes of poems for publication. Roy says that he knows Tagore "intimately," but he does not figure in Tagore's letters to any of the above-mentioned persons, or to those in the United States most responsible for introducing him there: Edwin Lewis, Harriet Vaughan Moody, Harriet Monroe, or George Brett, head of the New York Macmillan firm.[99]

The second undercurrent in the reviews, encouraged by wartime jingoism as well as by Roy's book, is that of nationalism. Roy does emphasize Tagore's cultural nationalism as manifested, for example, in advocacy of the use of the Bengali language. But Roy goes on to leave the reader with a stronger impression of Tagore as "Poet of Indian Nationalism." He describes Tagore's nationalism as humanistic and universal, but any reference at that time to an Indian as a nationalist was certain to serve as a springboard from the literary to the political. The writer for the *New York Times* admired Rhys's discussion of Tagore's educational theory but at once quoted Roy on the subject of government interference with Tagore's school and rebuked Rhys for not making a political point: "If these and other statements [by Roy] to the same effect are accurate—and there seems to be no reason to doubt them—it would seem that Mr. Rhys, as an English admirer of Tagore, has missed an opportunity when he fails to mention and comment upon the attitude of the Government as it apparently deserves."[100] The *Boston Evening Transcript* noted that where Rhys stressed religion as a dominant influence on Tagore, Roy stressed patriotism: "It is because Tagore, without losing the essential spirit of the Indian character, has been able to embody the new aspirations of Bengali national life, that he stands forth as a leader."[101] For Roy to emphasize this subject without careful exposition of issues involved in the Partition politics of the first decade of the twentieth century— issues imperfectly understood today in the West—was irresponsible in the extreme. Wartime relations between England and India were exceedingly delicate, and it was only four years since Bengali nationalists had forced the Government of India to abandon its Partition plan and to move the administrative center out of Calcutta; it was only three years since a nationalist had thrown a bomb at Lord Hardinge, the Viceroy, as he rode into Delhi to celebrate the transfer to the new city to be built there. Therefore Bengali leaders, reviewers thought, ought not to comment on the war then in progress.[102] *The Spectator* objected to Rhys's inference that Tagore had foreseen the war: "But are we to draw a distressing comparison between Christians at war and Bengalis philosophizing and poetizing at peace, because Bengal is not Belgium?... [We doubt] whether Mr. Rhys and Mr. Yeats and the other Celtic poets who lionized the Bengali man of letters have grasped the inner significance of the gardenhouse at Bolpur, or realize whither the Neo-Hinduism of Bengal is drifting."[103] *The Athenaeum* also took exception to Tagore's moralizing on the war and the effects of Western materialism: "The strength of the West lies in its recognition of the primary fact that the human spirit, as we know it here, is wedded to the clay, and advances only by accepting all the terms of the bond."[104]

Tagore was never reticent about expressing his views on either materialism or misguided nationalism, East or West. These views were firmly set forth two years later, in his collection, *Nationalism*.[105] Coming directly from him, however, these had an authenticity and force that no second-person account could give them. Rhys's intention was frankly literary; as he had told Rothenstein, he did not want to appear to "minister to any cult," but "to get at the paradox of the lyric impulse which seems so egoistic, but is really so bountiful, pouring out its pleasure for all created things, and transcending the smaller self to attain the greater."[106] His book was frankly a labor of love; after its publication he told Rothenstein:

> You know Tagore,—and where he is strong and where he is weak,—as no one else does in this country, I imagine; and it is good to think that my book satisfies you at all. That it will not please, or convince, the critics who are inclined to disbelieve in his reality, his art, and the rest,—I know well enough. But, I felt obliged to write about him cordially,—one may even say, uncritically, —giving way to the delight in a poetry that surprised one out of one's ordinary lukewarm feelings for contemporary half-inspired verse and prose. So let it be![107]

Tagore was apparently pleased with the book, for Rhys refers to a "welcome letter of May 19th,—a relief to me, since my book must have seemed in some ways a very innocently unoriental attempt to dive into your wonder-world."[108]

The next major English-language study of himself and his poems was Edward J. Thompson's *Rabindranath Tagore: Poet and Dramatist*, which appeared in 1926, succeeding his study *Rabindranath Tagore: His Life and Work*, a much smaller book published in India in 1921.[109] Buddhadeva Bose in 1946 considered Thompson "so far the only reliable European writer on Bengali literature"; Tagore, however, was not pleased with the 1926 book and said so to Rothenstein.[110] Thompson had candidly taken into account certain changes in Tagore's situation: his time and energies were increasingly taxed by his foreign travels and his labors in establishing Visva-Bharati University at Santiniketan, and the war had driven a great wedge between pre-war and postwar literary sensibilities in the West. As Sujit Mukherjee points out in his study, *Passage to America*, the books that followed *Gitanjali—The Gardener, The Crescent Moon, Fruit-Gathering, Lover's Gift and Crossing*—received progressively less space in review columns, and the stereotype of Tagore as an Oriental mystic remained entrenched in the minds of Western readers. The editorial assistance and critical support of Yeats and Pound were gradually withdrawn; Sturge Moore remained, but his interests were in neo-classical drama, and although his idiom was compatible with that of *Gitanjali* it did not accord with the more colloquial idiom of postwar poets in the West. Rothenstein was increasingly unable to give as much time and attention to Tagore's affairs as he had formerly done, first because of his appointment as Principal of the Royal College of Art, then because of a serious heart ailment. The declining interest of the general public is reflected in the ample and incontrovertible evidence of the sales and royalty records, now easily available to scholars in the various Macmillan archives. At the end of the 1920's Tagore was still a well-known world figure, but his later works were not being translated, or published by the Macmillans. The place once held by *Gitanjali* has been usurped by the non-literary pseudomysticism of Kahlil Gibran. Outside of scattered translations appearing in periodicals and anthologies, a few collections of translations by translators other than Tagore, and specialized works by scholars, his later works and hundreds of his earlier poems remain unknown to those unable to read Bengali.

CHAPTER 3

Tagore's Short Fiction

BENGALI literary historians generally agree that in their literature the modern short story began with Tagore's stories of the 1890's. No leading writer of Bengali short fiction (as distinct from the tale or short narrative) pre-dates him. Buddhadeva Bose says that Rabindranath "brought us the short story when it was hardly known in England."[1] Sukumar Sen says: "Tagore is the first writer of the true short story in Bengali (1891) and he has remained the best."[2] Bhudev Chaudhuri writes: "The Bengali short story had its first full flowering in the shelter of Rabindranath's work. Modern Bengali literature crept into an era of new experience with the start of Rabindranath's periods of short story writing."[3]

What makes the modern short story "modern"? It deals with what Frank O'Connor calls a "submerged population group": characters defeated by "a society that has no sign posts, a society that offers no goals and no answers.... Always in the short story, there is this sense of outlawed figures wandering about the fringe of society, superimposed sometimes on symbolic figures whom they caricature and echo—Christ, Socrates, Moses."[4] Thus the short story presents writers with all the problems of manipulating a multilevel narrative, and many readers fear it because it explores social and psychological areas that, consciously or unconsciously, they wish to keep hidden. The short story exposes these not as a panorama but as a single spotlighted experience of an individual. This experience, in relation to a lifetime, is usually very narrow in scope, but the proportions are reversed when it is seen in terms of that individual's outlook upon life. The short story spotlights a turning point, a moment of insight, an epiphany, after which that life will never again be what it was before. If the story is well written, and if the reader is perceptive, the reader"s life, also, will never be quite what it was before he read the story.

The modern short story not only makes the reader uncomfortable; it makes him work hard. "The short story," writes William Peden, "brief, elliptical, and unwinking, tends to ask questions rather than to suggest answers, to show rather than attempt to solve."[5] The modern short story is not really completed on the page; it achieves its final unity within the reader's conscience and imagination. It poses a problem, asks a question about it, and leaves the reader to fill in the missing piece of the puzzle, a piece often not found until long after he closes the book.

The genre was perfectly suited to Rabindranath's time and situation, for Bengalis needed to be forced to answer some urgent and vexing questions: what in Bengali life is worth keeping? What is to be discarded? What should replace that which is discarded? Tagore poses these questions again and again, in contexts of the interaction between society and the sensitive individual. These interactions, as they were presented in his stories, will be examined here under four headings: the tension between rural and urban elements; the tendency to misplace the value of English education; the influence of emergent nationalism; and the dilemma of Bengali women, who were already isolated by custom and convention, and were now perplexed by the storm of new influences that threatened the peace of the Bengali home. Rabindranath's stories are not invariably flawless examples of the writing of short fiction. He too often allowed himself to be drawn aside into philosophical digressions, distracting subplots, and misplaced whimsy. However, the manner in which his characters represent submerged portions of Bengali society, and his skill in asking questions about them, qualify his stories, on balance, as great examples of modern short fiction.[6]

I *Rural versus Urban*

The two major population groups most affected by the collision of British influences and Bengali traditions were the *bhadralok*, or "cultured people," whose chief common characteristic was that they did no manual labor and very often were landowners; and the *chotolok*, or "little people," among whom

were the *ryots,* or peasants. As the Permanent Settlement concentrated ownership more and more in the hands of the urban
bhadralok, absentee landlords who left their rural holdings to
the often careless attentions of overseers, the gulf between these
two groups widened. However, they had in common the fact
that they labored under certain disadvantages. The *chotolok*
lacked economic leverage and collective voice. The *bhadralok,*
who by birth and economic circumstances were better able to
move into the newly developing middle classes, often lacked a
balanced perspective. The cumulative blessings of education
retreated ever farther from the peasants, but the middle classes,
as they grasped at more than they could practically or gracefully
assimilate, did not care to be reminded that greater opportunity
carries with it greater responsibility, or that the search for en-
during values might well begin in the village. This was the theme
of some of Tagore's most important stories, and he reiterated it
almost to the day of his death. In 1940, he said this:

People often have homemade opinions about me. They say,
"He's such a wealthy fellow. He was born with a silver English
spoon in his mouth. What does he know of villages?" I can say
that those who talk thus know less than I do. How do they know
anything about it? Are they in the habit of getting to know villages?
To really know them is to love them. Maggots born in the bran
do not know the flower. They know that they find their satisfaction
outside it. I have seen village life with eyes which were invariably
loving. If it is said now that this will sound like vanity, then I shall
say that very few writers in our country have seen Bengal with
eyes which are sensitive to beauty. In my works there is an intimate
acquaintance with the village, and it will not do to neglect its
truth for some catchword. A happy attraction to those villages
awoke in my very youth; even today it has not left me.[7]

Examinations of the psychological distance between the *ryot*
and the urbanite, and even between rural and urban *bhadralok,*
appear again and again in Tagore's stories, of which three may
be considered here as being splendidly representative: "The
Postmaster" ["*Postmāstār*"] (1891), "The Return of Khokababu"
["*Khokābābur Pratyabartan*"] (1891), and "The Troublemaker"

["*Apada*"] (1895).[8] All three convey the message that not all of society's strengths are to be found in the Westernized society of the cities. Each of these stories brings a citizen of Calcutta into close contact with a person from the countryside, in a situation with possibilities for genuine communication; in each, for various reasons, the opportunity is wasted.

"The Postmaster" has particular importance as the first of Tagore's East Bengal stories to speak out clearly with the voice of Rabindranath, the writer of modern short fiction. The genesis of the story is well documented. At Shelaidaha the estate post office was in the Tagore house. The only circumstance transferred literally to the story is that the Shelaidaha postmaster was a lonely young man from Calcutta. In 1936 Rabindranath recalled that the Shelaidaha postmaster "didn't like his surroundings. He thought he was forced to live among barbarians. And his desire to get leave was so intense that he even thought of resigning from his post. He used to relate to me the happenings of village life. He thus gave me material for a character in my story: Postmaster."[9] To this rusticated young man, Rabindranath added details from the rural scene and a village orphan waif like so many he had observed during his travels from one part of the estate to another.

The Shelaidaha postmaster had Rabindranath to talk to. The fictional postmaster has no one:

Our postmaster belonged to Calcutta. He felt like a fish out of water in this remote village. . . .

The men employed in the indigo factory had no leisure; moreover, they were hardly desirable companions for decent folk. Nor is a Calcutta boy an adept in the art of associating with others. Among strangers he appears either proud or ill at ease. At any rate, the postmaster had but little company; nor had he much to do.

At times he tried his hand at writing a verse or two. That the movement of the leaves and the clouds of the sky were enough to fill life with joy—such were the sentiments to which he sought to give expression. But God knows that the poor fellow would have felt it as the gift of a new life, if some genie of the *Arabian Nights* had in one night swept away the trees, leaves and all, and replaced them with a macadamised road, hiding the clouds from view with rows of tall houses.[10]

For all his poetic notions about clouds and trembling leaves, the postmaster wants as little as possible to do with nature: "When in the evening the smoke began to curl up from the village cow-sheds, and the cicalas chirped in every bush; when the fakirs of the Bāul sect sang their shrill songs in their daily meeting-place, when any poet, who had attempted to watch the movement of the leaves in the dense bamboo thickets, would have felt a ghostly shiver run down his back, the postmaster would light his little lamp, and call out 'Ratan.' "[11] Ratan is the illiterate twelve-year-old orphan who is his housekeeper. In his utter boredom, exiled from the university circles of Calcutta to the only government appointment available to him, he begins to teach Ratan the Bengali alphabet. The reading lessons become the shining focus of her life.

When the postmaster contracts a fever she nurses him. As soon as he recovers he requests transfer to Calcutta. The transfer is refused, and he resigns from government service. Ratan asks him to take her home with him, to the mother and sisters he has so often described for her as a palliative for his own homesickness. He laughs off her request; it strikes him as so absurd that he sees no point in explaining his refusal. He commends her to his successor's care and on an impulse offers her his final month's salary. She refuses the gift and runs away to hide. As his boat departs, he has one more vague impulse: he will go back for Ratan. But the boat is caught up by the current; as it passes the cremation ground he soothes his conscience with platitudes about "life's many partings." After he has gone, Ratan wanders disconsolately about the post office, hoping in vain for his return.

This story was badly marred in the English translation.[12] Yet the story is so striking that, even in the flawed translation, even in spite of a few unnecessary digressions, its point is abundantly clear: the postmaster never realizes what he has done for Ratan by giving her the reading lessons. The human element in the teaching has had a value for her that he, with all his sophisticated literary education, is incapable of comprehending. Sorrowfully, the reader knows that he will never comprehend it, no matter how many civil service posts he may eventually fill, no matter how much he may circulate among

Calcutta's literati; the barely literate Ratan is far wiser than the postmaster can ever be.

"The Return of Khokababu" was Rabindranath's first story for *Sādhanā,* a journal launched by the Tagores in 1891. The central character of this story is Raicharan, a twelve-year-old village boy hired to look after the one-year-old son of a well-to-do couple. The son, Anukul, grows up, goes to college, becomes a lawyer and a member of the district magistracy. When Anukul's own son is born, Raicharan, now middle-aged, takes charge of him also. One day during the rains, when the Padma is over-flowing, Raicharan relaxes his vigilance for a moment, and Khokababu—an affectionate, playful form of address that means, roughly, "Mr. Baby"—disappears. Neighbors suspect gypsies or the river, but Anukul's wife suspects Raicharan has kidnapped the child. "'There was jewelry on him,'" she says, as she turns Raicharan out of the house. He returns to his village and marries, and after the birth of their first and only son, Raicharan's wife dies. At first he neglects the child because he feels guilty at having a son of his own. The more Phalna, his son, reminds him of Anukul's lost boy, the more the simple Raicharan is convinced that this is the lost boy reincarnated, and his former mistress' suspicions take on terrible new meaning for him. He begins to dress Phalna, even to the gold jewelry, as the lost Khokababu would have been dressed. When Phalna is old enough for college, Raicharan sells his bit of land, gets work in Calcutta, and puts his son, who is now thoroughly selfish and spoiled, into a student hostel. Neither father nor son mentions their true relationship to the boys at the hostel, who think, since Raicharan waits upon Phalna like a servant, that he is an old family retainer sent to watch over the son of the house.

Now the simple Raicharan returns to Anukul and his wife, who have had no more children. Raicharan says that he is indeed the kidnapper and will return their son. The boy he returns is, of course, his own. With great aplomb, Phalna accepts Raicharan's story, promptly and grandly accepts the role of a magistrate's son, tells Anukul that, to be sure, Raicharan has always behaved more like a servant than a father, and with cool condescension asks Anukul to give Raicharan a small pension. Raicharan offers a single explanation and defense: it was his fate that had taken

Khokababu, but, Tagore comments, "such an explanation can never satisfy an educated man." Raicharan departs alone, to "mingle with the uncounted persons of this earth"; the pension goes unclaimed; and Anukul, his wife, and Phalna continue—one must assume—smug in their conviction that justice has been done.[13]

"The Troublemaker" concerns a Calcutta man, Sarat, his wife Kiran, and his mother, living in a garden-house by the Ganges while Kiran recovers from an illness. A storm casts up from the river a half-drowned Brahmin boy, Nilkanta; he is an orphan who has been traveling with a *jātrā* troupe, wandering actors who perform episodes from the epics. Kiran and Sarat take him in, and Kiran relieves her boredom by showering Nilkanta with gifts. When Satish, her husband's brother, arrives from Calcutta for a college vacation, Nilkanta is consumed with envy, and a nasty undercurrent of animosity develops in the household. Then Kiran recovers, the family prepares to return to Calcutta, and Kiran suggests taking Nilkanta with them. The others oppose her, but no one says anything to Nilkanta about alternate plans for his future. He steals an elaborate German-silver inkstand that Satish has brought from Calcutta and treasures inordinately. Nilkanta denies the theft, Kiran defends him, then finds the inkstand in his trunk when she leaves him a farewell gift. He sees her there with the inkstand in her hand. He cannot explain that he intended to take it, not as a thief, but out of desire for revenge against Satish, and that he had intended to throw it in the Ganges but in a moment of weakness had put it into his trunk instead. On the last day of the family's stay, Nilkanta disappears, and it is Kiran, remorseful and ashamed, who steals out and throws the inkstand in the river. "Only Nilkanta's pet stray dog was left. It refused to eat and howled as it wandered back and forth along the riverbank."[14]

In these stories, without saying a word about educational theory, urban problems, or the need for rural reconstruction, Tagore has posed this question: if our education cannot open our eyes to human needs, what good is it to us? All three stories oblige the reader to fill in for himself the background of the Calcutta people. Tagore could assume that his readers knew it well, but he refused to assume that they knew how it was affecting them as human beings, and he insisted upon forcing them to spell out the consequences. The urban *bhadralok* in these stories have been exposed to the ideas conveyed by the "set books" that were required reading in secondary schools and colleges: Plato, Shakespeare, Wordsworth, Shelley, Keats, Byron, Tennyson, Browning, Dickens, Carlyle, J. S. Mill, Ruskin, Herbert Spencer, Thomas Huxley, Emerson and Thoreau and Balzac. Why, Tagore asks, have these powerful writers not done more to sharpen the sensibilities and sympathies of so many of the educated elite of Bengal? The postmaster is "astonished" when Ratan begins to cry and begs him not to ask the new postmaster to do anything for her; he has no inkling of how much the reading lessons and his companionship have meant to her. Anukul and his wife do not pause for even a moment to question or consider the magnitude of Raicharan's gift, and Phalna accepts them as his parents as thoughtlessly as he had always accepted all of Raicharan's sacrifices. Anukul—an arm of English law in India—decides that it is too late to look for evidence; he temporizes: "It would be wise to have faith."[15] When Nilkanta enters Sarat's household, the family think only of his benefit to them; Sarat's mother is delighted with the opportunity for acquiring heavenly merit by serving a Brahmin. Kiran's attentions to him are like the postmaster's to Ratan; he relieves her boredom, and despite her chagrin over the affair of the inkstand, she knows neither how much she has given to him nor the consequences of its withdrawal.

Tagore's fiction returns again and again to this theme of the thoughtlessness of the elite toward individuals whom they use and discard. They are not intentionally cruel, but cruelty is the inevitable result of their heedlessness. When they go to the country, they are restless, conspicuous misfits, with all the insulating assurance of the affluent. Yet it is their anonymous victims whom the reader remembers and who give these stories their power.

This pervasive sense of anonymity is functional in the narratives. It conveys, far better than pages of expository prose could do, Tagore's message about the nature of the rift between urban and rural Bengal. The *bhadralok* who identify themselves wholly with Calcutta hold the initiative throughout. Ratan, Raicharan, and Nilkanta are seen through their eyes, but their view is manifestly unreliable. In their scheme of things even the Brahmin Nilkanta is expendable. Almost there seems to be a general assumption that people whose standard of living falls below a certain level of comfort, who have no Calcutta connections, no college diplomas, are naturally unendowed with sensitivity or strong emotions. The irony, of course, is that Ratan, Raicharan, and Nilkanta stoically control overwhelming emotions that they cannot define, while the supposedly educated *bhadralok*, who have picked up all sorts of sophisticated definitions, do not recognize genuine emotion when they encounter it. They have lost in sensitivity whatever they may have gained in their ceaseless pursuit of the Bachelor of Arts diploma and the rupee. They do not know it, but of all Bengal's population groups, they are in danger of becoming the most deeply submerged.

II *Education-as-Wealth*

Utilitarian philosophy, embodied in the Permanent Settlement of 1793, made precise distinctions between public and private rights, with land as the basic standard of wealth and the state as universal landlord. "The British mind," says Eric Stokes, "found incomprehensible a society based on unwritten custom and on government by personal discretion; and it knew of only one sure method of marking off public from private rights—the introduction of a system of legality, under which rights were defined by a body of law equally binding upon the State as upon its subjects."[16] The crowning irony of the Permanent Settlement was that this attempt to stabilize English control over the Indian economy virtually guaranteed the impermanence of nearly all existing institutions in Bengal. Accumulation of property came to be regarded as the principal bulwark against the ravages of change, and property prerogatives became an obsession. In a great many Bengali stories, by other writers as well as by Tagore, one character after another seems to spend inordinate amounts of time and energy calculating, manipulating, bartering various liabilities and assets, with a degree from an English-language college heading the list of assets. Lost wills, stolen keys, forfeited gold jewelry, and iron household safes appear repeatedly. The

iron safe, in particular, might be the *machina* for the *deus* of
Bengali fiction—if it did not so often make its appearance empty.
As fictional devices these pieces of property were overworked,
but they are by no means merely evidence that Bengali writers
were poverty-stricken in imagination. As story plots often
depended on the management of property, so also did the fate
of individuals in real life.

Tagore was deeply perturbed by the insidious effects of this
obsession with property upon attitudes toward education. The
feeling of joyous liberation with which so many young Bengalis
had greeted the opportunity for English learning was being
displaced by a cynical view of education as just another piece
of negotiable property. Three of his stories represent the variations of tone that he bestowed upon this theme: "The Atonement" ["*Prayaschitta*"] (1894), "Rashmoni's Son" ["*Rāshmonir
Chele*"] (1910), and "The Devotée" ["*Tapashwini*"] (1916).[17]
All three stories deal with the manner in which the new educational system has set tradition and innovation in conflict.

In "The Atonement," the protagonist, Anathbandhu, comes
from a country town, has somehow managed to marry the
daughter of a well-to-do Calcutta family and moves in with it
while he attends college. Unfortunately, he is one of those
persons who project an impression of great competence but
refuse to put it to the test. Anathbandhu skips his examinations
and is a drop-out after one year. His wife, Bindhyabashini, who
sees her husband in his image of himself and devotes all her
energies to preserving it intact, insists that they leave Calcutta
and live with his family, away from the slights, real and imagined,
of her Calcutta friends and relations. "Anathbandhu," says
Tagore, "had plenty of vanity but no self-respect. He had not
the least desire to return to the poverty of his own home. Then
his wife became a bit stubborn and said, 'If you don't go, I'll go
myself.' "[18] They go.

In the village Bindhyabashini adapts to the harsher life, while
Anathbandhu, who knows that his brothers must contribute to
household expenses, refuses to take a job. He parades himself
and his urban journalistic interests before the awestruck village
boys, then decides that his talents need wider scope: " 'It is
impossible to get a decent job these days without training in

England. I've decided to go to England; you go to your father's and make some excuse for collecting money,'" he says to his wife, who refuses to do anything of the kind.[19] When they go to Calcutta for a visit, he steals his mother-in-law's keys, takes the money from his father-in-law's iron safe, and departs in the night for England, leaving his wife to shoulder the blame and explain as best she can. When he cables for money, she sells her gold jewelry. Eventually the late-blooming scholar returns as an accredited barrister and a full-fledged imitation Englishman. Bindhyabashini is in a fever of ambivalence: "Her pride in him was increased all the more by her own feeling of unworthiness. She was ill with unhappiness and exalted by her pride. She hated non-Hindu customs; still, when she thought of her husband, she said to herself, 'So many people become sahibs these days, but no one else looks as proper as he does! He is like a real Englishman! There's nothing to show he's a Bengali.'"[20] But when a drowning accident removes the next in line as his father-in-law's heir, Anathbandhu becomes the prospective heir. If he has not eaten beef abroad he can be returned to caste and may take his place in the family succession. He lies glibly about his diet in England, and the cleansing ceremony proceeds, flawed only by the unexpected arrival of Anathbandhu's English wife. Tagore leaves the rest to the reader's imagination.

Kalipada, the protagonist of "Rashmoni's Son," is the antithesis of Anathbandhu. Kalipada, also, is from the country, but his family has had wealth in the past and is now held together by the hard work and will-power of his mother, Rashmoni. Just as Bindhyabashini preserves the illusions of Anathbandhu, Rashmoni preserves those of her husband Bhabanicharan, a good-hearted bumbler who lives on memories of bygone wealth. She is further burdened by a horde of lazy and indigent relations: "Their bed of roses under the huge Chaudhuri family tree had been well shaded, and the ripe fruit fell right into their mouths—they had never had to work for anything."[21] Kalipada, Rashmoni's only child, is at first thoroughly spoiled by his loving and permissive father, until a trifling incident opens the boy's eyes to the fact that his mother's harshness is the result of overwork, and his father's permissiveness is compensation for inability to

provide all that the lost wealth had given Chaudhuri sons in
the past.

The issue of this lost wealth hinges upon a lost will and a
resulting split in the joint family. Kalipada now resolves to win
a scholarship in a Calcutta college. He tells his mother, " 'If I
can't study in Calcutta, I can't become a real man.' "[22] He and
Rashmoni make every sacrifice toward this end. In Calcutta
Kalipada, overworked and undernourished, lives in poverty in
a damp basement and is the butt of cruel jokes by a wealthy
playboy student who lives upstairs surrounded by a crowd of
sponging sycophants. One of these jokes leads to Kalipada's death
in Calcutta. The playboy upstairs turns out to be his cousin,
son of the Chaudhuri brother who had substituted a forged
will for the genuine one, thus leaving Bhabanicharan with the
worthless portion of the family property. One rainy night after
Kalipada's death the genuine will is thrust through Bhabanicharan's window. Without Kalipada, the will has no value for
them. " 'I have no more needs,' " Bhabanicharan says, and he
tears up the will.[23]

In "The Devotée," the student is Baroda, who, like Anathbandhu, has no scholarly motivations but, propelled by his father
and relays of tutors, at least tries the examinations. After two
successive failures, Baroda persuades his father that the English
atmosphere is more conducive to study, and his father agrees
to send him to England if he gets a Bachelor's degree in India.
Baroda is about to try once more when he discovers that the
family carriage that takes him to school has been sold as an
economy measure. "It was not at all difficult for Baroda to walk
to school, but how could he explain this humiliation to others?"[24]
He leaves his books and disappears to become an ascetic.

Baroda leaves also a thirteen-year-old wife who, like Bindhyabashini, knows in her heart that her husband is not perfect and
therefore does her best to preserve the image of his perfection.
She too turns asectic, finds a guru who convinces her that her
husband is sitting naked in meditation in the Himalayan snows,
and runs her repentant father-in-law bankrupt by setting up a
free feeding station for wandering holy men. Her father-in-law
knows that few of those who come are authentic holy men, but
he tolerates them because she continues to look among them

for Baroda. After twelve years he appears, but in Western
clothes, in an automobile, as salesman for an American washing-
machine company. The story ends with his producing an illustrated catalogue from his pocket.

With a bantering, deftly satirical tone, Tagore makes his
point that the obsession with education-as-wealth has set up a
conflict between tradition and modernity, and that this conflict
is both destructive and unnecessary. Anathbandhu and Baroda,
in order to escape hard work and traditional duty to their elders'
expectations, capitalize upon the prevailing educational snob-
bery. Anathbandhu, when it appears likely that traditional ways
may operate to his advantage, cynically resorts to lies, deceit,
and hypocrisy in order to get back into the orthodox fold. He is
only caught out by the fact of his having flouted Western as
well as Indian tradition. Baroda, from the beginning obviously
more salesman than scholar, at least advertises himself unapolo-
getically in his true métier.

Kalipada's case is different, and Tagore changes his tone
accordingly. He drops the bantering note and shifts to a tone of
sustained sympathy for the simple, trusting couple beguiled by
society's assumptions about the power of a college degree. His
scorn is heaped upon the system, not upon the student and
certainly not upon his parents. Kalipada, out of loyalty to his
family's traditions, hopes that academic success will compensate
for all of their disappointments. "Rashmoni's Son," written
nearly a decade before a Royal Commission came to investigate
the appalling conditions under which Bengali students lived
while attending Calcutta University, is a true picture of those
who lived in shocking poverty in order not to further burden
their self-sacrificing parents. Many of the survivors could look
forward after all only to unemployment or to a job unlikely to
provide opportunity commensurate with the kind of education
received; one thinks of Tagore's postmaster, stuck in a minor
up-country civil service post. Yet even to be able to include
"B.A. Failed" in one's credentials was distinction of a kind, for
it signified that one had at least been admitted to a college.
Such a situation set up unendurable tensions in youths like
Kalipada. Baroda survives because he cheerfully discards both

education and tradition. But, Tagore implies, what becomes of a country made up of Barodas?[25]

Tagore's solution was a fusion of education and tradition, on the pattern of the forest schools of ancient India, in which a few students gathered around a teacher or guru in a forest retreat, to live and study together close to Nature, alternating study and inquiry with periods of meditation. The school at Santiniketan was Rabindranath's practical demonstration of this method updated. His theories of education, all harking back to the miseries of his own early schooling, display a lifelong consistency. In 1892 he wrote: "An unkind fate has ruled that the Bengalee boy shall subsist on the lean diet of grammar, lexicon, and geography. To see him in the class room, his thin legs dangling from his seat, is to see the most unfortunate child in the world.... That explains why, although many of us take the highest university degrees and write many books, we as a people have minds that are neither virile nor mature. We cannot get a proper hold on anything, cannot make it stand firm, cannot build it up from bottom to top. We do not talk, think, or act like adults, and we try to cover up the poverty of our minds with overstatement, ostentation, and swagger."[26] In 1926 he said: "For our perfection we have to be at once savage and civilized; we must be natural with nature and human with human society. The misery which I felt was due to the crowded solitude in which I dwelt in a city where man was everywhere, with no gap for the immense non-human. My banished soul, in the isolation of town-life, cried within me for new horizons."[27] This is the idea conveyed by the conclusion of "Rashmoni's Son." When Rashmoni says of the genuine will, "What good would it be?" and Bhabanicharan says, as he tears it up, "I have no more needs," what they really mean is that the death of Kalipada, besides taking away their son, has blotted out the new horizons that they might, vicariously, have glimpsed through him. They are banished indeed.

III *Nationalism and Politics*

Lord Curzon's Partition Order of 1905, instead of dividing Bengal, gave Bengalis a new sense of unity and common purpose;

whenever censorship permitted—and sometimes when it did not—they rushed into street processions or into print to protest the order. However, less conspicuous channels of protest were already in existence. Since 1885 the National Congress had been meeting regularly, and it gave more and more of its attention to discussion of ways to gain a larger role in management of India's national affairs. The Swadeshi (*swa,* self; *deshi,* national) movement, which increased in power and momentum after 1905, also increased Bengali nationalists' awareness of the need for closer communication between urban and rural groups, between *bhadralok* and *chotolok.* This need soon made itself felt in the writing of Bengali prose. Writers began consciously to jettison its overload of rhetorical decoration, in an effort to make it a more straightforward medium of communication, intelligible to all levels of society without insulting the intelligence of the most literate.

Tagore's story, "The Editor" ["*Shampadak*"] (1893), is a deliberate summons to better communication at the colloquial level and is probably a jibe at his own prose style, which in the 1890's had a highly literary flavor.[28] In "The Editor," the *jamindār,* or hereditary landowner, of a large rural estate sets up a newspaper and hires as editor a Calcutta man whose claim to literary fame rests on the composition of a few dramatic farces that he had hoped might be profitable enough to provide education and dowry for his motherless daughter: "I made up my mind to earn money. I was too old to get employment in a Government office, and I had not the influence to get work in a private one. After a good deal of thought I decided that I would write books."[29] In so doing, he neglects the daughter he intends to benefit and realizes that writing is not a lucrative profession. Therefore the editorship of the country paper seems a godsend. However, the *jamindār* of a neighboring estate launches a rival paper, and the Calcutta editor goes down to defeat. His sophisticated subtleties and sarcasms are no match for his rival's blunt colloquialisms.

This is again the rural-urban dichotomy, but with a new ingredient. The editor from Calcutta, like Tagore's postmaster, is defeated by the rural environment; with the postmaster it is a case of no contest. In "The Editor," the rural editor is the

victor because he commands the language and therefore commands the sympathies of his readers. "What [his paper] published was starkly naked, without a shred of literary urbanity.
The language it used was of such undiluted colloquialism that
every letter seemed to scream in one's face. The consequence
was that the inhabitants of both villages clearly understood its
meaning."[30] The Calcutta man's rhetorical victories are lost on
those he is supposed to represent: "The result was that even
when I won decidedly in this war of infamy my readers were
not aware of my victory. At last in desperation I wrote a sermon
on the necessity of good taste in literature, but found that I had
made a fatal mistake. For things that are solemn offer more
surface for ridicule than things that are truly ridiculous. And
therefore my effort at the moral betterment of my fellow-beings
had the opposite effect to that which I had intended."[31]

The story ends with the daughter regaining her father's attention and the father cured of his literary pretensions. This story
misses many opportunities to round out characterization and
contrast the editor's urban background with his rural experiences.
However, it had a message of utmost importance for those urban
bhadralok who, in the first flush of nationalist enthusiasm, felt
compelled to preach Swadeshi to the countryside, only to find
that even to the up-country *bhadralok*, not to mention the
peasants, their cultural pretensions were either ridiculous or
incomprehensible.[32]

The patriots' relation to the British was equally complex. The
nationalist had somehow to reconcile his strong and sincere
commitment to all that English literature represented in his life,
with the actions of individual Englishmen in India who fell
short of the standards set forth by their own greatest writers.
Englishmen in Tagore's stories are frequently depicted as either
fair-minded but cold and remote, or blunt and brutal. When
the John Bulls do appear, the satiric emphasis has a way of
sliding over onto the deficiencies of those Bengalis who try to
remake themselves on the British model.

This sliding satirical emphasis is a salient feature of "Cloud
and Sun" ["*Megh o Roudra*"] (1894).[33] The Englishman here is
a Joint District Magistrate with a booming voice, wretched
pronunciation of Bengali, a blustering manner, and creaking

boots (the appearance of an Englishman in Bengali stories is very often heralded by the creaking of boots). This Magistrate gets embroiled in the personal affairs of an estate manager and humiliates him in front of all his villagers.

The Magistrate's real antagonist is Sashibhusan, Master of Arts, Bachelor of Laws, and son of an absentee landowner strongly reminiscent of Debendranath Tagore, for he has "sent his good-for-nothing son to look after their small village estate."[34] Again we have a Calcutta-bred college graduate whose training has failed to endow him with social skills. Sashi is shy and speechless at public meetings; near-sightedness makes him frown, so that he appears arrogant. He retreats to the shelter of his English books; his only friend is the manager's ten-year-old daughter, Giribala, whom he tutors because her father and her brothers scorn education for females.

Sashibhusan, this unlikely candidate for courtroom success, proposes to launch a lawsuit in order to restore the dignity of the estate manager. The Magistrate has already apologized, but the more he and the manager try to persuade Sashibhusan to drop the suit, the more stubborn he becomes. "Sashibhusan the bookworm, ignorant of the ways of the world, thought it not altogether impossible even in these mercenary days to perform the wonderful feats of orators like Demosthenes, Cicero, Burke, Sheridan, etc., who by the piercing arrows of their winged words had torn injustice to shreds, cowed down the tyrant, and humbled pride to the dust in the olden days. Standing in the small dilapidated house of Tilkuchi village, Sashibhusan was practising how to put to shame the arrogant English race flushed with the wine of victory, and make them repent for their misdeeds before the whole world. Whether the gods in heaven laughed to hear him or whether their divine eyes moistened with tears, nobody knows."[35]

He is so stubborn about the lawsuit that the Magistrate has begun to imagine sinister motives. "The Sahib's normal ruling-race complex led him to perceive clearly that this was all the Congress' doing. The myrmidons of the Congress were secretly going about everywhere seeking for opportunities to engineer trouble and write articles ... " He curses the Government of India for being too weak to give Magistrates summary powers to "crush these puny thorns underfoot forthwith. But the name of Sashibhusan the Congressman remained in the Magistrate's memory."[36]

This story has serious flaws. It opens with a long and heavily whimsical introduction of Sashi and Giribala, and with an extended philosophical analogy between their friendship and the interplay of cloud and sun overhead. Two principal plot lines concern Giribala's reading lessons and the lawsuit that interrupts them. The second plot collapses along with the court case, when the Sahib makes the manager an Honorary Magistrate, Giribala is married off, and Sashibhusan returns to Calcutta.

Now a third plot line is introduced in the form of a new crusade for Sashibhusan, who assaults the District Police Superintendent when a police launch gets into a dispute with a fishing boat. Sashibhusan's key witnesses again desert him to side with authority, and he goes to jail for five years. With a trite and highly melodramatic twist, this third plot is tacked onto the first; Sashi is rescued from oblivion by Giribala, now a well-to-do young widow. Nevertheless, the story is interesting not only for its echoes of "The Postmaster" and of Rabindranath's own experiences in East Bengal, but also for the demonstration of Tagore's technique for shifting the satiric emphasis from the Englishman to the Bengali. Here is a member of the intelligentsia, a logical leader of modern Bengal. His sympathies are sound, his education superior, but he is utterly incapable of striking a practical balance between his ideals and the realities of his situation. The story is the correlative of Rabindranath's 1892 essay: "We cannot get a proper hold on anything, cannot make it stand firm, cannot build it up from bottom to top."[37]

It must be noted, however, that the satire aimed at Sashi, while no less devastating than that aimed at the Sahib, has a lighter touch and is mixed with sympathy and a bantering tolerance and even affection. There is a much sharper edge to the satire in " 'We Crown Thee King' " ["*Rājtikā*"] (1898).[38] Tagore comments here that Bengalis who tried to be imitation Englishmen ended by not knowing what it was that they really wanted. One of two brothers-in-law, Pramathanath, has spent three years getting a Bachelor of Arts degree in England but is now cured of his infatuation with English ways. The other, Nabendu, longs for the British-bestowed rank of Rai Bahadur. Pramathanath, the "England-returned" brother-in-law, is supported by his three sisters and by another brother-in-law, a lawyer. They trick Nabendu into making a large contribution to the Congress. As a result, he is not listed as Rai Bahadur on the Queen's Honours List, but his in-laws receive him royally.

Tagore has set up the weaknesses of those who ape the masters and proceeds to shoot them down like clay pigeons. First, there is the traditional pattern of following caste and family custom; in Nabendu's case this has meant bowing and scraping for offcial favors from the British. His father had done the same, and "the youthful head of Nabendu Sekhar began to move up and down at the doors of Englishmen, like a pumpkin swayed by the wind."[39] Then Tagore sets up the contrast between Englishmen in India and the English at home. This was borne in on Pramathanath when, newly "England-returned" and a government-approved Bengali, he had left a railway car in sympathy with another Indian ordered out by a British police- man. The officer tells Pramathanath not to leave; he is first flattered, then realizes that he is like a well-trained donkey, for "the respect I receive is not given to me, but to the burden on my back."[40] He goes home, burns his English clothes, and avoids Englishmen thereafter. Third, Tagore aims a telling shot at the Congress by pointing out that merely enrolling names and col- lecting money is not true patriotism. When the Congress conven- tion delegates give Nabendu an ovation for his contribution, "our Motherland reddened with shame to the tips of her ears."[41] This story, like "Cloud and Sun," misses a number of oppor- tunities to sharpen both plot and characterization, but it does make its point: Bengalis who look to the Congress for ego- enhancement may as well get it from the British, for all the good they do either side.

This theme recurs again and again in Tagore's fiction, his novels as well as his short stories. In the short story "One Night" ["*Ekrātri*"] (1892), he warns of the dangers of stirring up enthusiasm for which there is no continuing guidance.[42] In "Broken Ties" ["*Chaturanga*"] (1916), a very loose-jointed novella that is really four short stories, he reminds readers that ideas as powerful as those of the Utilitarian philosophers are not to be lightly turned loose.[43] In "The Rejected Story" ["*Namanjur Galpa*"] (1925), he comments sharply on the public's appetite for tabloid stories as a substitute for genuine patriotic activity.[44]

As a group, Rabindranath's stories that deal with Bengali nationalism *per se* do not show him at his best as a writer of short fiction. He was almost always more effective when dealing with individuals than with mass movements. Even in *The Home and the World*, Bengali nationalism is reduced to personal terms so that instead of a tract the reader is presented with the concurrent diaries of three individuals who are memorable as personalities rather than as representatives of a movement.[45] Wherever his stories become more tract than fiction, their literary quality tends to decline. If this is a limitation upon his scope as a writer of fiction, it is consistent with Tagore's view of any nationalistic movement: it defeats its own purpose when it becomes more important than the individuals it professes to benefit.

IV *Women and the Community*

Tagore's fiction is filled with characters through whom he spoke eloquently on behalf of those whom the cultural revolution was forcing into silent isolation. Of these, his women characters are most memorable. When he writes about them, the bantering note is for the most part absent. In its place there is a corruscating irony, poured out upon the community as a whole for its failure to make full use of the talents of Bengali women. Most terrible of all is the ever-present implication that for every such fictional character, there are hundreds and thousands like them, living in psychological outer darkness that is caused, witnessed, and disregarded by a society so deeply submerged in material concerns that it has no surplus energies for concern about those unable to keep up with the pace of change.

If Tagore's women characters can be said to share a common characteristic, it is that even with their social disabilities, they are, as a group, stronger than the men. When Rabindranath theorized about woman's role in Indian society, his style tended to become flowery and inflated.[46] But his fictional women live and breathe. Bengali fiction drew strength from his depiction

of them, and Bengali society relied upon their simplicity and
sincerity, their powers of endurance, the integrity of their commitment to home and husband. The home could be restrictive
and the husband weak and vacillating, but women like Rashmoni and Bindhyabashini seem to move through the stories
by some force independent of the author's hand. When they are
on the scene, plots become tighter, and diction takes on the
straightforward cadences of workaday speech, so that dialogue
seems quickened in pace and immediate in tenor. The women
characters provide a continuing counterpoint of saving routine
that holds the social fabric together in the midst of shocking
and sometimes catastrophic events. While the men try inef-
fectually to cope with these, the women go steadily about their
timeless activities of cooking, serving, praying, waiting for someone to bring news from outside, or for some solution or miracu-
lous deliverance. One example may be taken as typical of the
dozens of such characters, some of them quite minor, in Rabindranath's stories. When Haralal, protagonist of "The Tutor"
["*Māstārmashāi*"] (1907), is unjustly accused of having stolen
his company's cash funds and is being taken away by the English
manager of the firm

his mother stood in their way and said, "Sahib, where will you
take my boy? I've starved myself to raise this boy. My boy would
never touch that money."
    The sahib did not understand Bengali. He said, "All right, all
right."
    "Mother, why are you upset?" Haralal asked. "I'll come back
as soon as I've seen the manager."
    The mother said in distress, "You haven't eaten anything all
morning."
    Without replying Haralal got into the carriage and went away.
The mother fainted and lay there on the floor.[47]

This vignette of personal and social tragedy tells the whole
story: the mother who has sacrificed every comfort to give her
son the education that would enable him to get a foothold in a
profession; the gulf between her and the son's English employer,
as wide and as deep as the sum of all the misunderstandings
between India and England; the impossibility of her crossing

over from her world of meals lovingly prepared, to his world of business affairs where inconceivable things could go wrong without a moment's warning; her utter aloneness with her fright and incomprehension; and her son's inability to comfort her.

Tagore gave Bengali men no rest from his criticisms of their backwardness in understanding the minds and hearts of Bengali women, an inevitable deficiency when so many women from the privileged classes spent their adult lives secluded in the inner rooms of the home. His admiration for those who, despite this handicap, fought on to get some education is always plain, and the Tagores practiced what he preached. Satyendranath had created a major scandal by taking his beautiful and talented wife driving unveiled in an open carriage in Calcutta, by having her taught in both Bengali and English, and by taking her with him to England. An older sister, Svarnakumari, was a leader in programs for training *zenana* teachers, who went to Bengali homes to instruct women who lived in strict *purdah*.

Still, Rabindranath did not idolize Bengali women in his stories, for rattle-brained females appear as well. The hero of the story "Bride and Bridegroom" [*"Pātra o Pātri"*] (1917) gets a Master of Arts degree, becomes a successful businessman, and is thus a prime target for marriageable young ladies and their mothers.[48] But now he is too particular to be easily caught, even though he is welcomed at a house where he was formerly excluded as unendowed and therefore ineligible:

But when I became prosperous, I not only had tea at that house, but ate lunch there, and after dinner in the evening played whist with the daughters and listened to them gossiping in their own distinctive brand of the English language. My difficulty was that I had been trained in English by reading *Rasselas, The Deserted Village*, and Addison and Steele. My achievement was nothing beside these girls'. "Oh, my! Oh dear, oh dear!" and similar elucidations did little to explain things to me. With my limited education, I commanded at the most a grasp of English that enabled me to make market transactions, but if the conversation of love had to be carried on in this twentieth-century English, my love would run away.

Yet they spoke a Bengali so famine-stricken that Bankimchandra himself would have been done out of the words for a pleasant conversation.[49]

Tagore's attitude toward these "Anglicized dolls" and their senseless conventionalisms is consistent with his attitude toward all cultural importations, namely, that whatever was imported should be fully understood and put to none but appropriate uses. The women for whom he shows sympathy and admiration are generally unsophisticated, patiently acquiescent in their isolated role, until some drastic change in family circumstances brings them up short at the realization of an intolerable situation. In three of his most powerful stories of this type, the heroines lack the experience and the means for dealing fully with crises in their relations with their husbands. They cannot go back to the old basis of marriage, but neither do they know how to go forward to something new that will command the husband's understanding and participation. Harasundari, of "The Girl Between" ["*Madhyabartini*"] (1893), keeps her husband, but her future life is an emotional desert that is doubly dismaying because she has glimpsed a promised land. Charulata, of *The Broken Nest* [*Nashtanir*] (1901), a novella, loses her husband, and the desert she faces is both emotional and intellectual, for she has discovered the joys of literary creation but cannot pursue them without her husband's support and approval. Mrinal, of "A Wife's Letter" ["*Strir Patra*"] (1914), leaves both home and husband, but only for the refuge of an ashram.[50] In all three stories there is an abyss between generations as well as between the sexes. The added weight of senior authority, so crucial in Indian society, makes the isolation of these women even more soul-destroying.

There are no would-be Oxonians or anglicized Calcutta dandies in "The Girl Between." The story has only three characters: Harasundari, a middle-aged wife; Nivaran, her husband, a stolid, conscientious clerk for an English firm; and Shailabala, a young girl whom he marries as a second wife after Harasundari undergoes a long illness that convinces her she will never have a child. The institution of a second wife, or co-wife, was condoned in Bengal in the 1890's; it made possible an extra dowry and sons to carry on the family name. However, many references in Bengali stories less explicit than "The Girl Between" bear witness to the family strife that was the price of this extra security.

"The Girl Between" is the story of a middle-aged woman's belated realization of how much she has missed in her youthful relation with her husband. When she survives her illness, she wants to do something wonderful, something exceptional to repay Nivaran for all his "lovingly disorganized nursing." It occurs to her that he might marry again. "She wondered why wives got so upset at this idea; it would not be at all difficult. Why was it impossible for one who loved her husband to love also a co-wife?"[51] Nivaran laughs off the suggestion, but then he begins to picture a home filled with children. He demurs, however, at having to bring up a girl-wife. The childless Harasundari, whose daughter, if she had had one, would be about the age of the new bride, promises to do all the bringing up, and Nivaran marries Shailabala.

At first, Nivaran avoids his second wife. Harasundari tries every ruse to bring them together. When she gives up in despair, Nivaran becomes interested and soon not only spends more time with Shailabala but neglects his office work to be with her. With each passing day Shailabala becomes more spoiled and selfish. After twenty-seven years of marriage Harasundari begins to see what she herself has never received from Nivaran; what weighs most heavily upon her is the realization that this emptiness in her life is not new: it has always been there. Only the realization of the emptiness is new. "It now seemed to Harasundari that someone had kept her from knowing the true meaning of existence. . . . Women are indeed meant to serve, but they are also meant to be queens. In the process of sharing, one woman had become the servant and the other the queen. But the servant had lost her pride and the queen was not happy."[52]

Shailabala is surfeited with attention. Nivaran is both unhappy and terrified, for he has been taking small sums from his company's till in order to buy presents for Shailabala. Harasundari knows where certain missing household funds, at least, have gone, and when he asks her to let him sell some of her jewelry, she asserts herself at last and refuses to give it to him. Instead, she herself gives it all to Shailabala, who "only knew that the normal course of all attention, all wealth, and

all good fortune would eventually lead to her because she was
Shailabala, she was the darling."[53]

Nivaran's embezzlement is discovered, and his employer sets
a deadline for the restoration of the two and a half thousand
rupees. Frantically Nivaran again asks for the jewelry, and
Harasundari refers him to Shailabala, who says that the jewelry
is hers, and that Nivaran's troubles are not her affair. "It dawned
upon Nivaran that the fragile little girl was more stern than the
iron safe. Harasundari was full of disgust at her husband's weakness in such a crisis."[54] Shailabala's contribution to the contre-
temps is to throw the key to her own iron safe out of the window
and into the pond.

Nivaran sells their home in order to replace the money. He is
not prosecuted, but he loses his job. "Of his movable and immovable belongings, only his wives remained. Of these, the
distraught younger wife became all the more immovable by becoming pregnant."[55] They move into a tiny house in a damp lane,
Shailabala falls ill, and despite Harasundari's devoted nursing,
Shailabala dies. "After gathering a world of adoration and affection, this little girl's life was pointlessly wasted in utter misery
and discontent."[56] Very soon Nivaran realizes that she "had
been his hangman's noose."[57]

Neither he nor Harasundari knows how to cross the gulf between them. "It was as if a bright and beautiful but cruel little
knife had cut his heart in two and had left a grievous line of
demarcation." One night he slowly goes to Harasundari's bed-
room. "Neither Harasundari nor Nivaran said a word. They lay
side by side as they had lain before, but precisely in the middle
slept a dead girl, and neither of them could pass over her."[58]

The double marriage, bizarre as it may seem now, is by no
means the most shocking aspect of "The Girl Between." The
story is shocking because it strikes so close to a mark that is
altogether outside the sociological fact of community approval
for one man's having two wives simultaneously. An emotional
discovery like Harasundari's is always a shock because it is a
solitary experience, and there is no external cure for the bleak
sense of time and opportunity forever lost. This sense of loss
is underscored by an aspect of this story that is unusual in
Bengali domestic fiction: the impression of Harasundari's literal

aloneness in the house. Stories about a Bengali home almost
always seem to be filled with people—servants, in-laws, widowed
aunts, indigent uncles, gossiping neighbors, officious Brahmins:
all the personnel of an Indian joint family household. But in
"The Girl Between" the house seems virtually empty. Nivaran
has a neighbor with whom he gossips in the evening, but after
Harasundari falls ill he stops going to the neighbor's house.
After Shailabala comes into the house, the stage becomes progressively more empty, and after they move from the old home,
ties with that neighborhood are cut. Servants, relatives, or
tradesmen may come and go, but the reader is unaware of them
because they have no place in the real action, which is an interior
action of the emotions.

That interior action proceeds in counterpoint. When Harasundari is ill and weak, Nivaran is not exactly strong, for he is
fumbling and ineffectual, but he is steadfast in his concern for
her. He is unimaginative and never guesses at the emotional
grounds for her plan for his second marriage. When Nivaran
becomes weaker and increasingly unrealistic as he succumbs
to its complications, Harasundari becomes stronger, and she
takes control of the situation—paradoxically—by giving Shailabala
the jewelry and then withdrawing. Is this passive aggression on
Harasundari's part? She must know that sooner or later Nivaran
must ask again for that jewelry. By shifting the responsibility
onto Shailabala, Harasundari shifts the onus as well. But Shailabala is secure in her selfishness. It is Nivaran upon whom the
onus alights because he is no match for Shailabala. The word
"nivaran" means "prevention," "restraint," "resistance." This
Nivaran goes down like a rag doll.

Just as he has collapsed at the wrong time, he exercises restraint at the wrong time. Harasundari knows that she has
encouraged Shailabala's selfishness by waiting on her. She
neither blames nor criticizes Shailabala. Nor does she blame
Nivaran, but she damns him by implication when she gives the
jewelry to Shailabala and thinks to herself, "But there was a
time when I was like you, and I too was filled to the brim with
youth. Why didn't anyone tell me about it then? That day came
and went, and I never even knew it."[59] "Anyone" is of course
Nivaran, the eternally unobservant husband who takes his wife

for granted. He is well-meaning but foolish, and two women are
sacrificed to his thoughtlessness.

Charulata, in *The Broken Nest*, is isolated in the midst of a
crowd; her household swarms with her husband's dependents,
her relations and their dependents, servants, tradesmen, and
visitors: all the population of a Calcutta joint family home. It
is the Tagores' own Jorasanko house reconstituted as the fictional
setting for another triangular family situation: Bhupati, the
middle-aged husband; Charulata, his young wife; and Amal,
Bhupati's young cousin, who lives with them while he goes to
college. The domestic stresses equal those of "The Girl Between,"
but the story goes farther and touches upon major dislocations
caused by English education in Bengal: infatuation with the
English language and literature at the expense of Bengali
journalistic aspirations and projects, nationalist sentiment, the
habit of measuring Bengali achievements by British standards
of excellence, and the conflict between tradition and innovation.
These are organized into two categories: the personal and domestic, and the literary. The categories interact throughout the
story so that *The Broken Nest* is both a tract for its time and a
study of fundamental human emotions under particular kinds of
stress.

In "The Girl Between," Nivaran, infatuated with his young
second wife, neglects Harasundari. There is no second wife in
The Broken Nest, but Bhupati neglects Charulata in his infatuation for something much harder to combat because it is inani-
mate: an English-language newspaper of which Bhupati is
editor-proprietor and to which he gives his virtually undivided
attention. Harasundari introduces Shailabala as compensation
for her own inability to have children. Charulata, unconsciously
casting about for some way of making Bhupati notice and approve of her, turns to the study of literature, a pursuit in which
she has Amal's help and encouragement. This completely changes
the basis of his participation in family affairs, and his companionship, which fills the void left by Bhupati's preoccupation
with the newspaper, becames more essential to Charulata than
she is able to admit. Amal does not die, but he is almost as con-
clusively removed: he marries and goes to England to study
law. Like Nivaran and Harasundari, Bhupati and Charulata

are stranded on either side of an unbridgeable gulf, with the thought of Amal everlastingly between them.

Both "The Girl Between" and *The Broken Nest* are stories of lost opportunities for love; *The Broken Nest* is also a story of arrested growth and wasted talents. Charulata in the course of her somewhat hit-or-miss studies reveals latent abilities as a writer; the irony of her situation is that even in her secluded life in *purdah*, she surpasses in achievement both her husband the editor and Amal the college student and would-be writer. Her talents have developed in a vacuum, except for the encouragement given by Amal—and that encouragement is withdrawn when he realizes that she has outshone him. She cannot go to lectures or literary societies; certainly no one even considers the possibility of her obtaining higher education. She cannot even go alone to a library, but must send a servant for books. She is terribly alone, yet she has no privacy. She is surrounded by people, yet there is no one with whom to share her distress over the break with Amal. When he leaves for England and she realizes the extent of the void left by his departure, she is confused by this "dangerous discovery... suddenly she found herself in this desert—days went by, and the wasteland kept growing more vast. She had known nothing about this desert."[60] She begins to lead an emotional double life: "Thus, in the unrelieved silent darkness where she had tunneled beneath all her household duties, Charu erected a temple to a secret grief and decorated it with garlands of tears.... She dropped all her household disguise at its door and entered in her true identity, and when she emerged she resumed the mask and appeared on the stage of worldly duties and pleasures."[61]

Bhupati knows at last where he has been delinquent: "But then, he had separated his life from hers—he had viewed her from a distance like a stranger, just as a doctor observes a dangerously ill patient. What powerful force had surrounded and attacked the heart of this weak girl? There was not a single person to whom she could have told all this, not a thing that could be told, not a place where she could open her whole heart and cry aloud—yet, while she carried this unspoken, unavoidable, insoluble, daily accumulating burden of sorrow, she had had to perform all her household chores like a normal per-

son, like her contented neighbors."[62] But Bhupati is too weak to
follow the lead of his understanding; he runs away from the
problem by going to another city to associate himself with
another newspaper. At the last moment, belatedly and half-
heartedly, he asks her to come with him. She is more realistic
than he: " 'No,' Charulata said, 'Let it be.' "[63] This is the last
line of the story.

Krishna Kripalani says that *The Broken Nest* and a full-length
novel, *Cokher Bāli* ("Eyesore": literally, sand in the eyes) (1903),
"laid the foundation of the modern novel in Indian literature."[64]
The heroine of *Cokher Bāli* is older than Charulata, widowed,
better educated, more experienced in the ways of the world, but
her emotions also cause domestic havoc because society allows
her no useful role and no scope for her intelligence and her
talents. In Tagore's novel, *The Home and the World,* a nationalist organizer insinuates himself into a home where he cynically
plays on the wife's emotions and on her longing to know more
of the outside world. In this case her weaknesses are offset by
the fact that he is an outsider, by his being a man of questionable
ethics who ends by being thoroughly discredited, and by the
husband's good sense. The damage to the relations of husband
and wife is finally repaired.[65]

But it is different with *The Broken Nest*. The damage is
irreparable, and Amal is not discredited. The subject is a particularly touchy one because it is related to a Bengali tradition
that rationalizes a necessarily strict social taboo. Kripalani says,
"The problem assumes special interest in the context of the
Hindu joint family where tradition has always permitted a tender
and affectionate familiarity between a married woman and her
husband's younger brother [or, as in Amal's case, a cousin-
brother]. In fact, the customary Indian term indicating this
family relationship (*devar,* derived from Sanskrit) means, literally, a second husband. Whether levirate or any other primitive
practice has kept its odour in this word is for anthropologists
to discuss."[66]

Anthropological considerations remain in the background of
"The Girl Between" and *The Broken Nest*. In "A Wife's Letter,"
Tagore pursued farther the themes of lost opportunities for love
and for development of women's talents. The story is less

satisfactory as fiction, for it lacks unity of place and thus loses the full impact of the claustrophobic confinement that is so important an element in the other two stories. "A Wife's Letter" introduces social issues more overtly and thus has more of the flavor of a tract; characters sometimes seem subordinate to thesis. But the thesis is no less powerful for being more obvious. It raised a storm of protest when it first appeared in 1914. As in *The Broken Nest*, the central action takes place in a home that swarms with people who seem either oblivious of the other inmates or at cross-purposes with them. Mrinal, the wife of the story, writes poetry, but, unlike Charulata, she has neither her husband's amused tolerance, nor anyone else to take an interest in her writing, much less in her reasons for making poetry her refuge. There is a younger wife in this story also, but she has a husband of her own, and the manner of this marriage precipitates the crisis of the story. The forces exerted on the two wives are external, not internal as in "The Girl Between." The point of the story is that Mrinal and the younger wife, Bindu, cannot cope with the pressures of society as it was then constituted. Bindu commits suicide. Mrinal lives to write her letter to her husband, but her victory is pyrrhic.

Mrinal reviews the fifteen years of her marriage as if they were—and they are—a story whose particulars are unknown to her husband. She makes it clear that she does not contemplate suicide as an escape: "Dying is not in my fate. I sat down to write this letter in order to make you fully comprehend that fact."[67]

She begins then to cite facts, with commentaries attached: each points to an entire aspect of Bengali culture. She knows that as she writes, her husband is at his office: "Calcutta is to you what the shell is to the snail; it has been fastened tight to your body and your mind."[68] She and a younger brother had had typhoid at the same time; the brother died, but she lived: "Yama [the god of death] is a canny thief and covets the things that are really valuable."[69] She was a village girl; her husband's family sought her as a bride because they had heard of her beauty, and the mother-in-law was determined that the second son should have a bride as beautiful as the eldest son's is homely: "Hope lies in the girl's beauty, but if she boasts none of that beauty, those who have come to look her over will pay whatever they think she is worth."[70] Her beauty is soon forgotten, "but the fact that I had intelligence rankled in your minds.... In an unwary moment God had given me more sense than was necessary for a housewife in your family. Can I return it now to someone else? Morning and evening you called me 'precocious girl.' "[71] She turns to writing poetry in secret: "That I am a poet is something you haven't discovered in all these fifteen years."[72] Mrinal's daughter dies soon after birth, and Mrinal loses the chance to be valued by the family: "I would have ascended directly from second daughter-in-law to mother."[73] Nor would she have minded dying along with her daughter; only those who have known affection mind dying: "A Bengali girl dies at every word. But is dying so brave a thing? I am ashamed to die; dying is all too easy for us."[74]

Bindu, an orphaned sister of one of the family's daughters-in-law, comes to the house. Bindu has been shoved aside by one relation after another, and Mrinal takes her into her own room to live. Bindu is homely, gawky, and graceless, and the family, including Bindu's sister, tries to get rid of her. Mrinal's spending money is cut off, and she deprives herself in order to keep Bindu. At last the family "resorted to the god of marriage" and found a bridegroom for Bindu. " 'If the groom is good,' answered Bindu, 'how could he be chosen for me?' "[75]

The bridegroom is not good. He is insane and has spells of violence. His family is as glad to get a caretaker for him as Mrinal's is to dispose of Bindu. She escapes and returns to Mrinal, who confronts the family with facts they have known all along. The homely eldest sister-in-law says, " 'Her fate is a bad one. What shall I do about it if it gives her trouble? Certainly, he may be mad, he may be a goat, but he's her husband."[76]

Bindu is sent back and runs away again to a cousin, but, as Mrinal's younger brother reports, " 'they were furious and sent her right back to her father-in-law's. They are still burning over having to pay damages, a fine, and cabfare for her.' "[77] The word "burning" soon acquires hideous meaning. Mrinal plans to go on a pilgrimage. Her brother is to put Bindu on the same train, but he appears alone, with the news that she has committed suicide by setting her clothes afire.

That was that. Peace reigned.

The whole population was incensed. People began to say that girls' setting their clothes on fire had become a fad.

You all said, "This is all playacting!"

That may be so. But why this stage stunt should be performed upon the saris of Bengali girls and not upon the dhotis of Bengali heroes is another matter that ought to be explained.[78]

"A Wife's Letter" is flawed by a drawn-out ending that works variations on the theme of Bindu's victory over death, and the story ravels out in philosophy and repetition. To the extent that Mrinal is left facing an uncertain future, it is a valid open-ended conclusion, but as in "Cloud and Sun" the ambiguity at the close lacks a function if the point of the story has been left behind. Mrinal drove that point home when she demanded to know why, if setting oneself afire was a stage stunt, it was performed only by Bengali women: this is one of Tagore's most devastating passages.

As a social document, however, the story is immensely powerful. It is plain that Mrinal's husband will not greatly mind or even notice for very long that she is gone. Tagore's critics who were so affronted by this story had had equal grounds for complaint in 1893 when his story "Punishment" ["Shāsti"] was first published.[79] In this story a man kills his wife in a fit of temper, and his brother puts the blame onto his own wife, saying to the Brahmin who happens in on the scene: " 'Sir, if one wife goes I can get another. But if my brother is hanged, I certainly can't get another.' "[80] But "A Wife's Letter" appeared in 1914, not 1893, and if Bengali wives were still considered expendable, it was an embarrassment to have this pointed out in print by Asia's first Nobel Prize winner.

V   *The Balance Sheet: Tagore's Short Fiction*

Three major collections of Tagore's short fiction in English translation appeared during his lifetime: *The Hungry Stones and Other Stories* (1916), *Mashi and Other Stories* (1919), and *Broken Ties and Other Stories* (1925). These made their way from India to the West under several serious handicaps. In the first place, the image of Tagore the guru-poet cast its enervating shadow upon them almost before they had left Macmillan's presses. Critics who in 1916 were no more enlightened about the cultural contexts of his stories than in 1913 they had been about the sources of his poems, now used the spiritual abstractions and the exotic settings, which had made the English *Gitanjali* so attractive, as excuses for not grasping firmly the nettle of constructive criticism. Since this demands of the reader that he have done some thoughtful homework, and since in the intervening three years neither general public nor professional critics had done much homework with respect to understanding India, both British and American reviewers of Tagore's stories tended to beg the question by wandering away to that stock-in-trade of imperial exchange, "the Indian mind." Once a critic had weighed in with the idea that "the singularity of the Indian mind lies in its emotional, not intellectual gifts," it became easy to avoid close literary analysis of the work at hand and to dismiss it by saying, for example, that "the big event [in *The Hungry Stones and Other Stories*] is the revelation by an Indian of Indian modes of feeling."[81] Or, a Kiplingesque dichotomy was invoked: "Sir Rabindranath Tagore's medium is not prose fiction.... Several of these stories take us into eternity, and these are better than the lighter tales, for certainly the humor of the Bengali is a little thin or too lacking in something to touch the Western mind."[82] Or, like a reviewer for *The Dial*, critics fell back upon the unfamiliar and noted that Bengali custom and usage "are to readers of our part of the world rather confusing than otherwise... Still, the thing that makes the book remarkable (and it certainly is remarkable) is not that it is Indian, but that it is very human."[83] But such reviews seldom testify to a careful examination of the particular human—and therefore, universal—characteristics that make the stories remarkable. "These stories are, if the word may be pardoned, more Tagoreish than any of the author's other previous writings," wrote the critic for *The North American Review*. "The author, one feels, does not know or care whether the story he is relating is romance or realism or merely a nursery tale."[84] The reviewer, one feels, does not know or care to search out whatever cultural reasons may exist for this vagueness of literary intention, or even to define his term "Tagoreish."

Similar evasive actions characterize reviews of the other two volumes. If it had not been preceded by *Gitanjali, Chitra,* and *Sādhanā,* said *The Times Literary Supplement, Mashi and Other Stories* "would scarcely have won paper and cloth and the labour of the press in days when all are as scarce as now. The implication is that the author of them—so few years ago a morsel for epicures!—is now a writer of fashion. Well, no matter what he puts forth in English, he cannot cloud the memory of the joy that rose from the first readings of 'Gitanjali' nor detract from the beauty of 'Chitra.' " *The Hungry Stones* had been "full of suggestion, of 'mysticism,' as we loosely call it," but *Mashi* was "much more on the surface of life."[85] *The Athenaeum* found *Mashi* "mostly shorter and slighter" than *The Hungry Stones* and "thoroughly Hindu in colour and feeling, and will be best appreciated by those who can place themselves at the ethnic point of view."[86] *The Bookman* made a stab at the "ethnic point of view" by saying that the contents of *Mashi* were subtle and sensuously appealing, suggestive of Japanese landscapes.[87] *The Nation,* less benign than *The Nation* in London, dismissed *Mashi* with the comment that, "reduced to bold yet often not quite idiomatic English, his artlessness, which may for all we know be charming in the original Bengali, seems labored."[88]

By 1925, when *Broken Ties and Other Stories* appeared, reviewers had generally abandoned even these tentative efforts at analysis. In the title novella, the *Manchester Guardian* found only esoterica of environment, conventions, and caste, meaningless to Europeans.[89] *The New York Times* spoke very kindly of Tagore's work as a whole, and of this collection in particular, but took the now well-worn escape route of saying that the stories "are not to be gathered under one formula or discussed in terms of occidental criticism. To those who can make the necessary mental adjustment they will bring some of the mystery, the color, the strange mingling of culture and barbarism of the Orient, which neither Kipling nor Conrad has succeeded in conveying. Others will weary of them almost directly."[90] That many readers did weary is confirmed by the records of Tagore's steeply declining royalty receipts and by the Macmillans' increasing reluctance to issue his new translations as rapidly as they had issued those immediately following *Gitanjali.* Some of this

slowing-down of sales was undoubtedly attributable directly to
wartime and postwar economics, but one must still ask why so
many readers apparently declined to make the effort of the
"necessary mental adjustment" to the stories, in order to understand at least some of the workings of "the Indian mind."

CHAPTER 4

The Other Tagore

TAGORE is a fascinating subject for study because he himself
was fascinated by everything under the sun. "Looking back,"
he recalled, "on childhood's days the thing that recurs most often
is the mystery which used to fill both life and world.... It was
as if nature held something in her closed hands and was smilingly
asking us: 'What d'you think I have?' What was impossible for
her to have was the thing we had no idea of."[1] He never ceased
to wonder at the immense variety of things to be found in
Nature's hands, or to be enchanted by the possibility of the
next day's surprise, and the next, and the next...

This same enchantment of the new informed all of his interests
and his activities. At times he overdid it; then body and mind
rebelled, and he withdrew to the solitude of Santiniketan or
Shelaidaha, to recover and to propitiate his poetic Muse by
writing lyric poems until he felt ready to meet the world again.
Still, it was his unquenchable interest in everything that produced what Buddhadeva Bose refers to as his quantity, range,
and variety. "It would be trite to call him versatile; to call him
prolific very nearly funny," Buddhadeva wrote. "The point is
not that his writings run into a hundred thousand pages of print,
covering every form and aspect of literature, though this matters:
he is a source, a waterfall, flowing out in a hundred streams, a
hundred rhythms, incessantly."[2] Of the streams that issued as
other than lyric poetry and short stories, the principal ones have
grouped themselves as dramas, novels, and nonfiction writings,
especially letters, journals, and memoirs. At the same time, the
multiplicity of his interests could be a disadvantage, for out of
this diversity came many of the pressures that beset his international career. The fact is that he was a great originator of
principles and plans, but he was not a great administrator and
needed assistants at hand to look after practical details. He would

115

further complicate things at times by taking details impulsively
into his own hands; if the lines of responsibility became hope-
lessly snarled, he would cast them down and depart, saying that
he was after all a poet and therefore must not be expected to
know about such matters. Because this habit had significant
effects on the translation of his works and on his relations with
his publishers and his friends and sponsors in the West, some
understanding of the consequences is necessary if one is to
understand also the fluctuations in his popularity.

I   *The Dramatic Works*

Orderly enumeration of Tagore's dramatic works immediately
presents bibliographical problems, for he loved to revise, enlarge,
abridge, and otherwise re-work both themes and materials from
earlier works. Sometimes the reincarnations had new Bengali
titles, and sometimes the titles were changed for publication as
a translation, thus making matters even more puzzling for the
unwary bibliographer. For example, the short story "*Sesher Rātrī*"
(The Last Night) (1892) was translated as "Mashi" (which
means "Auntie") for *Mashi and Other Stories* (1918); it was
then re-worked as a play called *Grihaprabesh* (literally, house-
entry) (1925), which was translated as "The Housewarming,"
for *The Housewarming and Other Selected Writings* (1965).[3]
Sometimes these were experiments with tone: comparison of
"Mashi" with "The Housewarming" easily makes apparent this
difference between the piece of short fiction and the play, whose
plot was adjusted so as to facilitate insertion of several *Rabindrasangit*. Sometimes these metamorphoses were a simple transfer
from one genre to another, as when the satirical story "*Karmaphal*"
(literally, fruit of action) (1903) was dramatized as *Sodhbodh*
(Final Settlement [of Accounts]) (1926), which was translated
as "Consequences" for *The Housewarming*.[4] And sometimes they
were experiments with form, as when the story of the verse-
drama *Chitrāngadā* (1892) was retold as the dance-drama
Nrityanatya   Chitrāngadā   (Dance-Drama   Chitrangada)
(1936).[5] (In English translation the verse-drama was published
as *Chitra* [1913], which is also the title of a volume of Bengali
poems [1896].)[6]

These examples are cited, not to confuse the general reader, but in order to emphasize the creative restlessness of Tagore's imagination. He not only experimented with genres and with combinations of genres new in Bengali literature of the theatre—prose drama with songs interspersed, verse-drama and dance-drama with songs—but with social commentary through drama. His play *Prayaschitta* (Atonement) (1909) is an adaptation of his first novel, *Bau-Thākurānir Hāt* (The Young Queen's Market) (1893), given twentieth-century immediacy by the addition of a character who is, as Kripalani points out, "the prototype of Mahatma Gandhi and anticipates the latter's campaign of non-violent civil resistance and non-payment of taxes as the people's answer to the tyranny of an unjust ruler."[7] Gandhi had not yet appeared on the national scene; the play is Tagore's reply to nationalists who criticized his withdrawal from the Bengali anti-Partition movement. He further experimented by making his plays the actual embodiment of social experiment and protest: although dancing was associated by ancient tradition with prostitutes and was therefore not an art to be learned by girls from respectable families, Tagore trained girl students at Santiniketan as dancers, and they appeared in his dance-dramas, not only at the school but in Calcutta.

The Tagore *Centenary Volume* lists forty-one Bengali dramatic works of various kinds published during Tagore's lifetime; six of these are revisions, abridgments, or enlargements upon earlier dramas; fourteen (one published posthumously) are re-workings of earlier poems, short stories, novels, or plays. Only nine of his dramatic works were published in English translation while he was alive, eight of these appearing between 1913 and 1917. Five more, translated by others after his death, were published between 1950 and 1961; one of these was for private circulation in India, and three were special Centenary publications. In addition, George Calderon adapted Tagore's story *"Dāliyā"* (1892) as a play called *The Maharani of Arakan*, produced in London in 1912 and seldom seen since that time; Sturge Moore thought the adaptation "all out of keeping."[8]

The Macmillan archives contain a not inconsiderable amount of correspondence, principally from England and the United States, about permission to produce Tagore's translated plays.

This correspondence follows the curve of popularity of his other works: after 1920 there is a steep decline. This decline is, in part, a consequence of new and inevitable directions in drama on both sides of the Atlantic as the influence of Ibsen and Shaw made itself felt. Lyric drama, hieratic acting, and epic themes in epic contexts were overborne everywhere by more prosaic idioms, except among scholars, litterateurs, and those eager to sample an atmosphere foreign to that of their native land and literature. These, in general, were and are the audiences for Tagore's plays. John Masefield, one of the first friends to whom Rothenstein sent the manuscripts of Tagore's plays, read them with interest and pleasure but replied that in his opinion "the plant won't transplant." The plays were too brief to hold the interest of Western audiences; the dialogue was of a kind un-congenial to Western actors; staging would require a delicate touch beyond the abilities of Western directors.[9] What Masefield rightly described as delicacy was in many cases the result of a play's having been written for production out of doors, for audiences of Santiniketan schoolboys for whom stylized ritual and epic allusion were a part of everyday living.

Tagore's gentle parable, *Dākghar* (Post Office) (1912), trans-lated as *The Post Office* (1914), was produced by Yeats's Abbey Theatre players in Dublin and in London. These, wrote Ernest Rhys, had been "perhaps as near a bid at the Indian stage illusion as one can hope to get under the circumstances.... Judged by a London standard, it may seem that all [Tagore's] dramatic work is lacking in ordinary stage effect, but·to this criticism one can only reply that his plays were written to attain a naturalness of style and a simplicity of mode which only Irish players have so far realised for us."[10] The consensus of London reviewers was that the Irish group had failed to create the Indian illusion. Those who went to the Court Theatre expecting a comedy set in an Irish post office, noted the reviewer for *The Globe,* must have been surprised to find "the members of the Abbey Theatre Company in the white garments of the East,... Play is scarcely the right name for 'The Post Office,' which is really a poetic and conversational fragment, with no pretence to anything approaching drama.... One likes it or one does not. For ourselves we found it impresive, but thought it too

tender, too ethereal a thing for the theatre."[11] *The Standard*
called it a "dream play," and "a pathetic fantasy" that was
charming but could not be called dramatic.[12] *The Evening
Standard* called it "an allegory which is barely definable."[13] The
Times reviewer called it "dreamy, symbolical, spiritual . . . a curious play, leaving to a certain extent a sense of incompleteness,
since it ends before the climax, rich in poetical thought and
imagery, as well as in a kind of symbolism that must not be
pressed too closely." The cast tried hard to "represent Indian
natives [but] remained always Irishmen."[14] *The Westminster
Gazette* found it "one of those elaborate attempts to be simple
and elemental which are favoured by those who by non-com-
mercial drama mean drama that nobody would pay to see. . . . it
was all on one note and never moved one inch; and, looking
back on it, I cannot remember anything said by anybody to cause
it to go on even for the short time that it lasted."[15] This London
run lasted through three performances, on a double bill with
J. M. Synge's *The Well of the Saints.*

Thus Masefield was proved right, then and thereafter: the
plant has not transplanted well. But one must point out what
no one had apparently pointed out to the reviewers of *The Post
Office*: the play was written for Santiniketan boys, not for London
theatre-goers, and a number of Tagore's plays—most notably
Chitra, translated from *Chitrāngadā*— were closet drama, written
to be read or given reading performances, not to be mounted as
theatrical productions. Even the political dramas have this same
static quality, for they are allegories, parables, or thesis plays.
Tagore's Bengali diction in most of the plays is too ornate for
literal transfer into English, but it was stripped down more than
need be for the translations, and the result is line after line that
seems curiously exposed and vulnerable. Even in Bengal, Buddhadeva Bose wrote in 1948, productions of Tagore's plays had
not usually succeeded, and his influence upon the drama has
been inhibiting rather than encouraging; under his influence,
literature in Bengal had grown in subtlety while the theatre
remained "crude and conventional, depending much on players
and little on playwrights, . . . Our stage has a Tagore-fright which
it takes no trouble to conceal, and would sooner plunge headlong
into the Ganga than think of touching any of his symbolical

dramas."[16] Although Buddhadeva regretted that Rabindranath never tried to establish a repertory group in Calcutta (on the model, one imagines, of the Abbey Theater in Dublin), the fact remains that his plays are the plays of a poet, not amenable to rule by economic principles, in the West, or, one suspects, in Bengal.

II *The Novels*

Paradoxically, the Bengali novel is best known to the West today through the medium of film. Ironically, a poll of the audiences who have seen the three widely circulated, lyrically praised Satyajit Ray films based on the two "Apu novels" by the modern Bengali writer Bhibutibhusan Bannerji, would without any doubt prove that the vast majority of viewers in the West had no notion that these films are adapted from novels and not made from original film scripts.[17] Still less are they likely to have any orderly conception—or, indeed, any conception at all—of the precocious Bengali tradition out of which these novels and films have sprung.

The first great figure in the history of the Bengali novel was Bankimchandra Chatterji, that same personage who had honored the young Rabindranath with his garland.[18] His contribution to Bengali fiction and prose style, says Sukumar Sen, was that he "brought in imagination. . . . what Chatterji did was to break its [i.e. Bengali prose] monotony, shear off its ponderous verbosity and give it a twist of informality and intimacy. Chatterji's own style grew up as he went on writing."[19] The progress that he represented was relative, for his style, by present-day standards, was still very formal, his diction highly literary and Sanskritized, and it is a giant step from, in the words of Buddhadeva Bose, "Bankimchandra's stiff formalism to the diamond depths of Rabindranath's later prose."[20] Bankimchandra's novels read now like period pieces, "domestic romance with a moral underlining and a social motive."[21] But they are worth reading for their insight into Bengali domestic life in the latter half of the nineteenth century. Their social motives could be explosive, as in his novels *Bishabriksha* (The Poison Tree) (1873) and *Krishnakānter Uil* (Krishnakanta's Will) (1878), both of which dealt with widow remarriage, then forbidden by the strictest social and religious taboos.[22] Their appeal was soundly based on Bengalis' increasingly strong desire to read about themselves, to have a literature that depicted daily life as they knew it.

This was the cue that Tagore took from Bankimchandra for his ten Bengali novels published between 1883 and 1934. Three of these were translated into English for publication during his lifetime: *Ghare-Bāire* (At Home-Outside) (1916), as *The Home and the World* (1919); *Noukā-Dubi* (Sunken Boat) (1906), translated as *The Wreck* (1921); and *Gorā* (1910), translated with the same title, which is the name of the protagonist (1924).[23] Four more were translated after Tagore's death: *Dui Bon* (Two Sisters) (1933), as *Two Sisters* (1945); *Sesher Kabitā* (The Last Poem) (1929), as *Farewell, My Friend* (1949); *Chār Adhyāy* (Four Chapters) (1934), as *Four Chapters* (1950); and *Cokher Bāli* (Eyesore) (1903), as *Binodini* (1959).

Even if Tagore's novels, in their turn, strike the reader somewhat as period pieces, some of the characterizations are unforgettable. As in the short stories, one is struck by the vividness and the strength of Tagore's women characters. This is especially true of *Cokher Bāli*, whose heroine, Binodini, is a young widow who comes into a middle-class home and refuses to accept the restrictions upon what she feels is every woman's right to love and domestic happiness. Her situation is like that of Charulata, in *The Broken Nest*, insofar as Binodini knows that she possesses talents and great intelligence; her resentment and restlessness are fed by the realization that those talents will never be used, and her passionate revolt finally tears the family to pieces. "Half a century ago, when *Cokher Bāli* was first published, in the eyes of Hindu society, Binodini's image was appalling," Buddhadeva Bose has commented. "Then, one had to be really reckless to write this book."[24] Yet even Tagore, for all his recklessness, was intimidated by public opinion, for even the fiery Binodini capitulates at the end, to the great detriment of the novel. She tells the man who really loves her and wants to marry her that marriage is impossible: "'The very thought of it is shameful,' said Binodini. 'I am a widow and, besides, a woman in disgrace. I can never allow you to lose caste on my account. Please, don't ever again utter such words.'"[25]

Similar motifs and evidences of social restrictions appear in

the three novels translated between 1919 and 1924, and their
timing was not auspicious. The war was over, and English
liberals clamored for belated reforms, among them women's
suffrage, liberalized divorce, and property inheritance laws. Im-
perialists of an evangelical bent could easily interpret such episodes in Indian novels as proof that English rule had not yet
delivered India from a benighted state, and therefore the Englishman must not lay down that burden just yet. Readers who
held such views would have been quick to notice that the plot
of *The Home and the World* was centered upon an episode
typical of abuses within the Swadeshi movement, which was
even then causing the Government of India no end of trouble,
and upon an unscrupulous organizer for that movement. They
would not have known—for the copyright page of the translation gives no hint of it—that *The Wreck*, written in 1906, was
well on its way to becoming a period piece, but they would be
quick to note that it dealt with a young woman victimized
by a restrictive society. And *Gora* was a study of the relation
between Hindu orthodoxy and Indian nationalism. This is by
no means to suggest that the novels should not have been translated and published, but one must say that novels like these bore
a very heavy responsibility, coming at such a time from a writer
of such prominence. He became even more prominent in a new
way in 1919, the year of publication of *The Home and the World*,
when he resigned his knighthood as a protest against the Amritsar Massacre.[26] In 1920 he began a frenetic series of international lecture tours in support of his plan for a center of international studies at Santiniketan. This tour presented an excellent
opportunity to support the novels with a series of lectures
carefully planned to explain their literary and social contexts,
and incidentally to help Macmillan to publicize them. However, Tagore left both the books and the publishers to shift
largely for themselves. He stayed only briefly in England in
1920, then rushed away to America for a disastrous tour punc-
tuated with disappointments and exhaustion. In 1921 he again
visited England only briefly, hastening away this time to the
Continent for a whirlwind lecture tour that caused a break-
down in his health and led to the rupture of more than a
year's duration in his friendship with Rothenstein.[27]

The reviews of the novels reflect this progressive loosening of the lines of communication. In the more liberal journals *The Home and the World* was received as a gloss on current events that was both practical and poetic. "Sir Rabindranath Tagore," commented *The Saturday Review*, ". . . has succeeded in raising the social and political ferment of modern India to the high poetic plane with the least suppression of the truth, but force of vision."[28] The New York *Nation*, which on occasion had been less than gracious toward Tagore's works, found *The Home and the World* "a profoundly wise and beautiful book."[29] *The New York Times* pronounced it "a quaint, interesting and significant book, a curious blend of informal narrative, satire and poetry. Its characters are all here in New York, and in London, and in Chicago and in Medicine Hat, as well as in India . . . a disarmingly innocent satire."[30] The satire was certainly not intended as innocent, but this review represented a more serious error. Sujit Mukherjee, who has made a detailed study of the American reviews, finds repeated indications that reviewers believed that Tagore wrote these novels in order to interpret India to the West.[31] One can understand, however, that such an impression might gain currency, since Tagore himself was then traveling in the West. Furthermore, when *The Wreck* appeared in 1921, it not only bore no date of Bengali publication but was not identified as a translation. Mukherjee notes that although it received the longest American review of any work by Tagore (2,350 words in *The New York Times* for June 26, 1921), "it may be held responsible for ruining any prospect he might have opened with his first English novel." Mukherjee finds the incident that motivates the plot patently a manufactured one, and "a large portion of the author's energy is spent thereafter in repairing the cracks in the credibility of the initial accident, while several other chance circumstances are required to bring the story to successful fruition."[32] Western readers of *The Wreck* simply had no way of knowing what many Bengali critics agreed upon even then: in the decade from 1906 to 1916, between *Noukā Dubi* and *Ghare Bāire*, Tagore's Bengali prose style had grown enormously in flexibility and in colloquial flavor; he had apparently been heeding his own advice set forth years earlier in "The Editor."[33]

If the longest American review of Tagore's work dealt with
The Wreck, the most significant review of any of the novels
was that of *The Home and the World* by E. M. Forster, which
appeared in *The Athenaeum.* This review, together with his
1914 review of *Chitra,* was reprinted in *Abinger Harvest* and
thus eluded the relative transience of periodical publication.
Forster attends to first things first: he judges the quality of the
writing, not as an item for export or import, but as a literary
question. He finds it wanting because of "bad tastes that verge
upon bad taste" and because of a persistent strain of "vulgarity."[34]
The bad tastes are caused by sentences that Forster found highly
inappropriate to the theme and therefore inept and ludicrous,
and he quotes one that is disfigured by a disastrous shift in tone.
He calls it a "Babu sentence"—a sentence that aims at subtle
satire and sophisticated commentary but overreaches itself and
ends up sounding ridiculous. What Forster had no way of knowing was that the damage was done in the translation and that
for the Bengali reader the Bengali sentence had had the correct
delicate balance between sophistication and vulgarity.[35] Vulgarity—behavior that reflects an inability to recognize values and
virtues—is the theme of this novel. It is embodied in Sandip, the
cynical opportunist who becomes a Swadeshi organizer and insinuates himself into the affairs of a landowner and his naive
wife, whose emotions Sandip shamelessly manipulates for the
enhancement of his own ego. Forster calls Sandip a "West Kensington Babu," which sums up the character of a bourgeois
schemer who, by attaching himself to the fringes of a legitimate
cause, imagines himself to become thereby a great man. What
Forster means is that Sandip is not evil *enough.* If he is not to
be an Iago, he must be an Iago *manqué,* like the slipshod Verloc
in Conrad's *The Secret Agent.*[36] If Tagore had weighted the
whole emphasis of his novel toward the meanness and shoddiness of Sandip, the shallowness and petty pretensions of the
"West Kensington Babu" would have been appropriate to the
story, as Verloc's shoddiness is appropriate to *The Secret Agent.*
But the emphasis in *The Home and the World* is weighted toward
the theme of a sheltered Indian wife's inability to cope with the
intrusion of militant nationalism. Because Sandip as a foil for
her is inadequate, Bimala, the wife, falls short the standard

for heroism set by Winnie Verloc or even by some of Tagore's own heroines—Harasundari, for example, of "The Girl Between."[37] This misplaced emphasis, Forster says, produces the literary vulgarity of the novel, for Tagore has dealt with the kind of "hackneyed situations from which novelists are trying to emancipate themselves in the West." Failure does not deter Bengalis, says Forster, because "they have interest in the constitution of the world."[38] If Bengali novelists were somewhat behind Western novelists in refinement of literary techniques, Indian readers would find the novel decidedly up to date: the anti-British sentiment of which Swadeshi was the expression—however it might be conveyed in novels—*was* a product of Indian nationalism. *The Home and the World,* whatever its faults as fiction, demonstrated the consistency of Tagore's view that positive ends never justify negative means. Unfortunately, the literary shortcomings of his translated works forfeited the attention of some intellectuals in the West who were sympathetic both to him and to Indian nationalism. *Gora,* when it appeared in English in 1925, was virtually ignored in America and got very little attention in England.[39]

Gora belongs to the same vintage as *Noukā Dubi,* for it was begun in 1907, while anti-Partition protest was at its height and Tagore smarted under the criticism of those who called him a turncoat for his failure to approve the terrorism of the extremists. *Gora* is his effort to analyze in his retirement at Santiniketan, the significance of Indian nationalism as it relates to the clash between old and new, between rigid orthodoxy and free inquiry. Gora is an Irish foundling, raised by a kind Brahmin woman after his parents were killed in the Sepoy Mutiny of 1857. He knows nothing about his origins and grows up a fanatic proponent of Hindu orthodoxy in its most reactionary forms. The discovery, after he has created havoc in the lives of several close friends, that he was born neither Indian nor Hindu and is thus totally outcaste, makes him reverse his views so that he becomes an exemplar of Tagore's ideal, the Universal Man.

Gora as an English translation labored under two initial handicaps. The hero's fortuitous circumstances inevitably reminded readers of Kipling's *Kim;* Tagore was not flattered by being regarded as an Indian Kipling. And Gora talks too much. The

long disputes and colloquies in the novel are Tagore's way of
working out ideas that had great urgency in 1907, but by 1925
readers in the West were accustomed to less static novels, and
the mood of the West had passed the point of intellectual inquiry into the rationale of Indian nationalism.

III   Non-Fiction Prose

Tagore's essays, lectures, sermons, and instructional writings
cover an enormous range of subjects. Much of this material has
not been translated and is therefore inaccessible to readers who
do not know Bengali. Some of it, such as the sermons delivered
at Santiniketan, would require a great deal of annotation for
foreign readers and even then might appeal principally to students of Eastern philosophies. But a number of collections of
essays and lectures with more general appeal have been published and have achieved wide distribution. Among these are
Sādhanā: The Realisation of Life (1913), papers presented in
Urbana and elsewhere in the United States in the winter of
1912–13; *Personality: Lectures Delivered in America* (1917),
on a wide range of subjects, both abstract and concrete; *Nationalism* (1917), on nationalism in the West, in Japan, and
in India; *Creative Unity* (1922), essays and lectures, many of
them on aesthetics; and *The Religion of Man* (1931), his 1930
Hibbert Lectures at Oxford. In 1961, in observance of the Tagore
Centenary, eighteen of his Bengali lectures, on education and
India's role at home and abroad, were translated and published
as *Towards Universal Man*. A fair sampling of his literary criticism will be found in *A Tagore Reader*, also a Centenary publication.[40]

The personal writings that give a more intimate, more relaxed
picture of the man and his personality made their way westward
more slowly. His *Reminiscences* did not appear in an English
translation until 1917.[41] Other writings—journals, diaries, letters—
have become available sporadically, but there are vast amounts
of such materials still untranslated from Bengali and still unpublished in English. It is a pity that this should be so; for readers
who never had the opportunity to see him in person, such materials provide a more accurate and just impression than that
projected by the stereotype of the wise man from the East.

There can be no doubt that he made a profound impression upon those whom he met during his travels. Many of Rothenstein's friends echoed his admiration for Tagore.[42] And the impression did not fade. Miss Mollie Cohen, who had been a student, then an instructor at the Lewis Institute in Chicago, then Assistant and Associate Professor of English after the Institute became a part of the Illinois Institute of Technology, recalled seeing Tagore at the Institute during her student days nearly half a century before:

Yes, I did meet Tagore and his son and daughter-in-law. . . . When I learned that he was in Chicago and staying with the Lewises, I begged Dr. Lewis to bring him to read his poetry to us. A few days later, all the language and literature students and professors, mostly two in a seat, crowded into our large classroom to listen to Tagore speak in his elegant English and read from his poetry. He ended by reading from an as yet unpublished manuscript of a play . . . Afterwards, some of us joined him and his son and daughter-in-law in Dr. Lewis' office for a very brief introduction.

The two members of his family were attractive enough. But Tagore himself made on all of us an unforgettable impression of extraordinary beauty. I can still see his dark, prophetic eyes, the smooth, silky grey hair and beard; I can still hear the oracular cadence of his voice. All the photographs that appeared at the time in various periodicals did him justice—except in the ambiance of his radiant presence, which, I suppose, can be attested to only by those who were lucky enough to see him.[43]

Jibansmriti (literally Life-Memory), Tagore's memoirs of his early years, had been published in 1912 and translated by his nephew Surendranath Tagore for serial publication in the Calcutta English-language periodical, *The Modern Review*, during 1916. Their publication by Macmillan as *My Reminiscences* (1917) came about in part at the instigation of Yeats. Although at the time Yeats was becoming more reluctant to continue editing any more of Tagore's manuscripts, he deduced from Rothenstein's reports of the memoirs that they might point "a moral that would be valuable to me in Ireland"—the moral to be found in Tagore's example as a leader of a thoroughgoing cultural renaissance.[44] Yeats wrote to urge upon Tagore the

idea that publication in the West would help his readers there
to "understand [your poetry's] relation to your country and history," and he suggested that such a book could have "political
importance."[45] Tagore replied that "few things would give me
greater pleasure than to have a part, however remote, in the
revival of Irish national culture." Unfortunately Surendranath
had not finished all the translation. Rabindranath feared also
that it was too limited in scope: "They deal only with my early
days and stop short about the age of twentyfive, so these reminiscences are more narrowly personal than anything else. . . .
My anxiety is that I may not give you any false expectations."[46]

If read in the light of the great changes in the art of biography
and autobiography that have taken place since 1917, Tagore's
Reminiscences do not come up to expectations. They are a
collection of sketches rather than a systematic recollection.
Chronology and notes are lacking, so that the reader who has
no supplementary information about Tagore has no steady point
of reference or clear idea about persons and events described.
The translation is pedestrian and often departs unnecessarily
from the Bengali text. Still, the sketches contain valuable descriptions of the ambiance of the Tagore home and family, of
the young Rabindranath growing up there, and of the ferment
and excitement caused in Bengal by the intrusion of new ideas
from the West. *Chelebalā* (Boyhood Days) (1940), another,
shorter memoir, translated by Marjorie Sykes as *My Boyhood
Days*, was published in India in 1940, but this merely supple-
ments the earlier, longer work and breaks no new ground.
There are no comparable memoirs for his life after the age of
twenty-five, and no complete, systematic autobiography.

The memoirs of childhood and youth are supplemented at
this point, however, by *Chinnapatra* (Torn Leaves [or, Letters])
(1912), translated by Surendranath Tagore and published by
Macmillan as *Glimpses of Bengal* (1921).[47] This comprises letters
and excerpts from letters written between 1885 and 1895 from
Rabindranath to his niece Indira Devi. "A number of my Bengali letters written in my young days had been collected some
years ago," he wrote to Yeats in 1918. "I was convinced that
they could be of great help to explain my writings which appeared unintelligible to some part of my readers. My nephew

Suren has translated these letters into English. They cover those very years which were most productive for me and therefore they act like a footpath in my life history, unconsciously laid by the treading of my own thoughts. I feel sure these letters, when published, will present to you pictures and ideas concerning me and my surroundings more vividly and truly than anything that I have yet written."[48] About this he was quite correct, for the letters have an immediacy that no recollection, however vivid, can have. They give the reader a direct insight into the Rabindranath of the early East Bengal years, which were indeed "most productive." People and places in his short stories and poems written there spring into luminous life as he observes and describes them from vantage points on the houseboat or on the shore. Unfortunately, the translation again is pedestrian, and in departing too often from the Bengali text it leaves out too many of the delightful and touching turns of phrase, and subtleties of syntax that make good writing even better.

In recent years *Chinnapatra* has been expanded in a new edition called *Chinnapatrabali* (also, Torn Leaves) (1960), for which 107 new letters to Indira Devi have been added, together with more complete versions of 145 letters from *Chinnapatra*. There are several collections of his letters written during various travels, ranging from his first visit to England, to his 1930 trip to Russia, and an important exchange with the Bengali musician D. P. Mukhopadhyay, on the subject of music. None of these collections, except the letters from Russia, is easily available.[49]

Tagore's letters written in English have particular significance in relation to his international career, since questions of his mastery of English frequently arose—often introduced, as has been noted, by Tagore himself. As one answer to this question, his letters to William Rothenstein have been published without alterations in Tagore's texts; these demonstrate that Tagore's English was very good indeed, even, as Mollie Cohen recalled, "elegant."[50] Prepositional usages gave him the most trouble, he felt, but this was evident principally when he wrote under stress; in general he used even those not only correctly but colorfully.

Two volumes of letters in English published in Tagore's lifetime have particular interest in connection with specific periods of his travels abroad. Both of these comprise letters to C. F. Andrews: *Letters from Abroad* (1924), a valuable commentary on Tagore's rather chaotic lecture tours of 1920–21, and *Letters to a Friend* (1928), which is *Letters from Abroad* revised and enlarged to include letters written between 1913 and 1922.

Like many great letter-writers whose correspondence was a means of conversing with distant friends, Tagore does not seem to have been a habitual diarist. But he kept diaries and notes during many of his tours abroad. During his lifetime there appeared Bengali editions of *Iurope-Jātrir Diāri* (Diary of Travels in Europe), in two parts (1891, 1893), accounts of his first visits to England; *Jāpān-Jātri* (Travels in Japan) (1919); *Jātri* (Travel) (1929), which combines accounts of the journey to South America in 1924 and to Java in 1927.

A volume of travel essays that would have answered many questions about Tagore at the turning point in his career was not published, even in Bengali, until 1939. This was *Pather Sanchay* (Travel Notes; literally, Collection from the Road) (1939). These essays were written in the crucial year of 1912, and they help to supply a perspective upon Tagore during his visit to England and the United States. Observers have recorded a great variety of impressions of Tagore as he appeared to them. Less well known, because less widely distributed, were Tagore's impressions of those whom he observed. How did England appear to him, on his first visit since 1890? Did he feel alien and uncomfortable in the West? How did he view friends like William Rothenstein, and the friends whom he met through Rothenstein? Did his observations form themselves into a pattern, or was he receiving merely disjointed impressions? Did he draw analogies between English society and Indian society? Above all, did he regard himself as a cultural alien in the West?

Essays in *Pather Sanchay* answer all of these questions. He found London a hostage to the motor car. "I had seen plenty of crowds in the London streets," he wrote, "but now motor cars posed a new obstacle. This embodied even more plainly the rush of the city. Motor-bikes, motor-buses, motorized goods carriers had been turned loose in a hundred streets to shake London. I thought, how terrifying to have this rush in every single street of London! How horrible if that were the external image of its mind! What a ferocious pulling and hauling about of time and place they carried on! Those who walked through the streets exercised extreme caution every day. No matter what else you turn your thoughts to, at the same time it is necessary constantly to adjust them to this varying motion. It would be dangerous to make a mistake.... Time for seeing, hearing, and thinking will beat a retreat here."[51]

In the first few days in London, he felt alien indeed. "But we cannot spend our days observing man merely as this machine," he wrote. "If I don't get to know him where he is a man, why have I come! But it is as easy to see man where he is a machine, as it is not easy to see man where he is man. There is no getting in if the man inside does not call us in himself. But it is not like buying a theatre ticket; there is no price on it—it is a priceless thing."[52]

Fortunately, he knew Rothenstein. But he had known him as a foreigner in India, where Rothenstein had caused some British eyebrows to be raised because he made it so clear that he had come to see India and Indians. His meetings there with Tagore had been comparatively brief; their meeting in London in 1912 was Tagore's first opportunity for observing him among his own countrymen. He quickly found the essence of Rothenstein's personality and the secret of his influence in the world of the arts: "He is a well known artist. A short time ago he came for a short time to India. In that short time he saw into India's very heart. Seeing with the heart is like seeing with the eyes—it is not a matter of analysis, nor does it require much time. As regards seeing with the heart, how many people spend their lives in India blind from birth; they have not seen that light of our country which, if seen, makes it easy to see everything else.... His greatheartedness is so freely manifested all the time that then and there [in India] my heart was strongly drawn to him. This desire to know him really well drew me more than anything else when I traveled to Europe."[53]

Rothenstein had felt compelled to make the most of every minute in India; Tagore in London felt the same: "The road from strangeness to acquaintance is very long. I had no time to go down that arduous path. My strength, too, was limited. Because it was always my way to stay in a corner, I could not even try to reach the coveted spot by shoving with my own strength into the crowd. Besides, I did not have the English language as key to the outer door; I had to jump over the fence—traveling is such a gymnastic feat: this sort of thinking did not liberate me from my own nature. If I had not had the opportunity of freely becoming acquainted with [Rothenstein], I would probably not have had the ability to become easily acquainted with others. Instead I would have worn myself out trying, for a short while, to survive the wheels of the devil's chariot here—the motor-car—and finally would have gone home, to the streams and winter rice fields under the shimmering autumn sunlight of my river-enclosed Bengal. Just then my friend appeared on the scene and raised the curtain. I saw a seat prepared, I saw the lights burning; a great burden was lifted from the unacquainted foreigner, the dust of the traveler was brushed away; in a moment's time I went from solitude into a company."[54]

India was always in Tagore's mind, and as he looked and listened among new friends in London, he continually drew parallels with people and institutions he knew in India. He described the Rothensteins' Hampstead house and garden, but it was the children who kept his attention:

When I sit on this veranda, happy with one book in my hand, I feel no need of reading another book. I am quite happy watching the outpouring of the unfailingly happy freshness of childhood in his two small sons and two small daughters. I see a profound difference between them and children in my country. It seems to me that we are the men of a very ancient time; in our country even the children seem to come into this world bearing the burden of antiquity on their backs. They are good, their movements are circumscribed, their big black eyes melancholy—they do not ask many questions, they seem to keep their conclusions to themselves. And all these [Rothenstein] children have been born into the provenance of a new age; they have been intoxicated by the taste of the newness of life; they will think and act entirely for themselves; therefore their restless feet will run everywhere, and their restless hands will touch everything. Undoubtedly the children of our country are naturally restless, but at the same time the heavy weight of anti-restlessness seems always to have kept them largely im-

moveable. The life of these [Rothenstein] children does not bear
that unseen weight but only sparkles as it dances melodiously like
a fresh spring.[55]

Others also, introduced by Rothenstein, started trains of
thoughtful comparison. One such person was Henry Massing-
ham, editor of *The Nation*, and Tagore was invited to attend one
of its editorial luncheon meetings. "*The Nation* is the principal
weekly paper of the Liberals here," he wrote. "In England all
those who are great persons do not judge native and foreigner,
their own class and other classes, by measurement against the
false weight of self-interest; *The Nation* carries the message of
those who do not wish to give shelter anywhere, on any pretext,
to unfairness, who are genuine friends of all men.

"The editor and writers of *The Nation* meet at luncheon one
day a week. Here they eat and meet each other and during the
meal discuss the articles for the next week. There is talk in
abundance; the writers for this top-ranking newspaper are all
extraordinary individuals with respect to knowledge and skill.
That day, as I look a place at their feast of talk I was filled
with joy.

"As I sat among them I repeatedly thought only that all of
them know that each is responsible for the truth. They do not
merely compose sentences; each of their essays pulls the tiller
of the British Empire boat at least a little to right or to left.
In such a situation a writer cannot make use of only his own
ideas. In our country there is no such standard among our news-
papers; we feel no responsibility toward our writers, and therefore the writers' powers do not escape from total laziness, and
work goes by the board. Thus our editors see no need to instruct
and exercise vigilance over our writers; these people write and
instruct readers undiscriminatingly. We are not cultivating the
field of truth because our budding shoots look so ordinary to
us—we have not planted a fully satisfying food for the mind."[56]

Rothenstein introduced him to H. G. Wells: "I had read a
book about American society and a novel or two by the famous
contemporary writer Mr. Wells. From those I learned that his
mental powers shone like a steel sword and were as sharp. When
my friend invited me to have dinner with him, I was somewhat

frightened. . . . At first I was nervous; then it appeared that there was nothing of the porcupine about the man; he was wholly affable. I saw that he was sharp in thought, but not in nature. In fact, he has a genuine feeling for mankind, a hatred of injustice, and devotion to the progress of Universal Man; if that prevails, men's minds will get no satisfaction from mere chatter. . . .

"I thought repeatedly about something else I had seen, of which I have spoken before. That is the quickness of their thinking. While my friend and I talked with Wells, the stream of talk continually shone with bits of glowing thought. Word after word threw off sparks; time flew. It was plain to me that their minds are on the alert."[57]

He met Stopford A. Brooke:

A copy of these translations of mine came into the hands of Stopford Brooke. He thereupon invited me for dinner one day. He is elderly, but I felt that his age transcended his seventy years. He had a kind of inflammation of his leg; getting about was very difficult for him. He sat with that leg up on a stool. Old age defeats and lays some men low, but with others it comes to a standstill and lives with them like a friend. Old age could not fly its victory flag over his mind and body. His youthfulness is amazing. It occurred to me again and again that when an elderly person looks youthful, he looks better than everyone else. And why not? That sort of youth is a matter of truth. . . .[58]

And there was Tagore's first impression of Yeats:

The poet Yeats was not lost in the crowd. One recognizes him as an outstanding person. He is so tall that his head towers over almost everyone, and it seemed to me when I saw him that he was fully involved in everything: the current of an artist's creativity was directed toward one point and gushed forth on all sides like a spring. That was why I felt that he was inexhaustible in body, mind, and spirit. . . .

The poet Yeats has set his own poetic stream flowing along Ireland's mythological path. It is entirely natural for him because he has earned there such extraordinary fame. He has clarified this world by his life, not with knowledge, but with his eyes. To do this, he does not view the world merely as a worldly thing; on its vast mountain expanse he feels existence to be filled with pleasure attainable through meditation. . . .

Everyone knows that for some time Ireland has been in the throes of an independence movement. This suffering suddenly became excessive because English rule weighed from all sides upon the Irish spirit. For a long time this suffering tried to declare itself principally as political rebellion. Finally something else was tried. Ireland realized her own independence of spirit and was ready to declare it.

On this occasion I thought of our own country. In our country also, for a long time an effort to gain political control has predominated in our educated circles. It became apparent that a great many of those who led this effort had no affinity with the language and literature, the customs and usages of the country. If they had to talk to the common people, there was no communication. They were for doing anything and everything to improve the country, entirely with the English language and English government. As for the people of the country who had to do the work of the country, the intellectuals did not glance in their direction.

But fortunately, in Bengal at least, we began to appreciate our own thought in literature. . . .[59]

Many of Tagore's countrymen had been frankly puzzled by his motives for this journey. Indians are reluctant to leave their homes and travel for any but spiritual purposes, he said in a lecture delivered shortly before he left for London: "After all, salvation lies in visiting holy places and peoples—in India." His purpose, he said, was ". . . simply to go. I am lucky to have been born on this earth and it will be real satisfaction to see as much of it as I can."[60] One hears in this echoes of his childhood sense of "mystery which used to fill both life and world," and Nature holding something in her closed hand and "smilingly asking us: 'What d'you think I have?' "[61]

He knew, he told his hearers in 1912, that there were points of conflict between India and the West. He recalled the hoary cliché that "European civilization is materialistic and soulless. That idea does not have to be supported by facts. What some say, others echo; numbers sanctify, and take the place of reason." He insisted that the West's achievements must have some measure of spiritual force behind them; that spiritual force was what he hoped to discover and define.[62]

The essays in *Pather Sancay* prove that he found it in the intellectual force embodied by men as different in personality as Rothenstein, Wells, Brooke, Yeats, and the editors of *The Nation*. The essay in which he describes his meeting with Wells is pointedly called "*Inglānder Bhābuksamāj*": "England's Society of Thinkers." Although later experiences were sometimes less happy, he never wavered in his belief that it was the individual with a world view and an understanding of the arts who made all the difference, in both East and West. Even at the end of his life, when he felt that his ideals of a lifetime were being laid waste by the second World War, he held to the hope promised in the lives of a few individuals who represented the best of what Western civilization had to offer.[63]

The Tagores had long been criticized for going more than half way to meet new influences from the West, and the essays in *Pather Sancay* would have confirmed the more orthodox in this opinion. But it is plain in the essays that India was always his frame of reference. Everything he sees, everyone he meets, all are placed in that perspective. Advantages and disadvantages are carefully weighed up on both side of the scale; if what he sees in England seems superior to its Indian counterpart, he praises in such a way as to clarify his thoughts about changes that would benefit India. If he sometimes prefers Indian to English values, he does not summarily reject all things English. He knew, he said on the eve of his departure, that he would meet paradoxes and puzzling contradictions, but "these are the hazards which make this journey a pilgrimage of truth. . . . Indeed it is the difficulties that make the journey worth while, for what is easily attained does not become a part of our being."[64]

Above all, these essays give a true picture of Tagore as he was in that crucial summer of 1912. He did not come to criticize or to pontificate. He was a quiet observer who saw everything with a fresh perspective; he collected and stored information and impressions, turned them over in his mind, and tentatively fitted each new experience into place. He enjoyed himself thoroughly among his new friends; they, as Rothenstein often said, delighted in both his wit and his wisdom. The solemn stereotype of saint and guru was of Western manufacture, and the eagerness with which it was fastened onto him says more

about the West's feelings of insecurity than about any that
Tagore may have felt at that time.

IV *Practical Matters*

That he did come to feel some sense of insecurity—or, at least,
disquietude—about his international role after 1913 is too often
stated in his letters to be disregarded.[65] It was directly related
to the multiplicity of his interests, for the responsibilities that
they brought him became more than one man could well dis-
charge, if he wished at the same time to preserve the uninter-
rupted hours necessary to a writer. It is ironic that his interests
as a writer—the role that had brought him to the world scene—
should be those to suffer. However, as he became more famous,
and at the same time more occupied with the work of his
school and with traveling and lecturing abroad in order to raise
funds for it, he left more and more of the work of translation
to others, and he himself was increasingly hard to find when
Macmillan editors had questions about details of manuscripts
and publishing schedules. The assistants to whom he delegated
these matters were devoted but were not always able to deal
adequately with them. As letters in the Macmillan archives
show, the difficulties that resulted had inevitable effects upon
both the books and sales—and sales were of great importance
because they were a principal source of income for the school
at Santiniketan.

The translation and production of Tagore's fiction, both the
short stories and the novels, illustrate the kinds of problems that
arose. The Macmillans, from the outset, had proceeded with
caution. When Rothenstein had proposed in 1912 that Macmillan consider issuing a trade edition of *Gitanjali*, George Macmillan had replied as follows:

We have now received a report from our reader on the poems
and other writings of the Bengali poet, Rabindra Nath Tagore, and
I am glad to tell you that he shares the favourable opinion of the
poems already expressed by other able critics. He thinks, however,
that it would be well to proceed by stages in bringing his work
before the English public. As you yourself pointed out to me, some
of the material which you left here after the printed volume [the

India Society edition of *Gitanjali*] is not as good as the rest and there would be need of careful selection. What our advisor suggests is that we should in the first instance bring out the India Society's volume in a more popular form and at a lower price, e.g. 4/6 or 5/– net and see how that takes. If it went off well it could be followed by another volume of verse carefully edited and possibly also a volume of dramatic dialogues. The collection of essays and short stories, which seems to be badly translated, he thinks might at any rate for the present be set aside.[66]

The Macmillan adviser who reported on the manuscripts was the journalist Charles Whibley, who knew not a word of Bengali and so could not possibly have known whether the works were "badly translated," so far as faithfulness to Bengali meanings was concerned; he could deal, therefore, only with the English wording of the translations. However, it stands to his eternal credit that he perceived the wisdom of proceeding "by stages." "A large volume of poems, delicate as these, would be an artistic mistake," he wrote to George Macmillan. "Here, indeed, the half is greater than the whole."[67]

Tagore's letters to the Macmillan firms, to Rothenstein, and to other friends, indicate that for all his acute perception of the role of the English intellectuals whom he had met, he never fully grasped the extent of his phenomenal good luck in Rothenstein's having secured for him the prestige and distribution resources of the Macmillans. Indeed, he treated this great gift with surprising carelessness, for which the only excuses can be the overload of work from his various activities and a natural distaste for the details of such business. He left these to others; until 1914 they were in the capable hands of Arthur H. Fox Strangways, the musicologist who was Secretary of the India Society. Without remuneration, he served Tagore as business and legal agent until the Nobel Prize made this work too much for him. It was Fox Strangways who had hammered out with the Macmillan firms the excellent contracts that brought Tagore, over the years, a foreign income in the tens of thousands of pounds and dollars. The responsibility of acting as Tagore's agent was then given to the London Macmillan firm (at a fee of five percent instead of the customary ten paid to a professional agent), but many of the negotiations from Tagore's side fell into the hands of C. F. Andrews, who, as the letters in the various archives show in great detail, did much damage to the very valuable relationship between Tagore and his publishers.

Tagore's own expectations were at first very slight. "I am so glad to learn from your letter that my book has been favourably criticized at the Times's Literary Supplement," he wrote to Rothenstein from Urbana in 1912, after the India Society edition of *Gitanjali* had appeared. "In fact, I feel that the success of my book is your own success. But for your assurance I never could have dreamt that my translations were worth anything and up to the last moment I was fearful lest you should be mistaken in your estimation of them and all the pains you have taken over them should be thrown away."[68]

What *was* thrown away was a possibility of orderly procedure in the preparation of successive books, thus freeing everyone's energies for closer attention to the quality of the translations. "By the bye," Fox Strangways wrote in 1914 to Brett, head of the New York Macmillan firm, "these people who approached you with permission to deal on behalf of Mr. Tagore. I think you should ask to see their power [of attorney]. I did not know that he had executed any *power* besides the one I have, though it is quite possible he has. But he has given verbal leave in a light-hearted way to all sorts of people to do what they have a momentary or a real wish to do."[69] Evidence of this kind abounds in the Macmillan archives: Tagore continued this unsystematic procedure despite warnings from Fox Strangways and the Macmillans of the dangers to his own interests. He began to expect that his books would be always published at the same rapid pace. He misjudged both the influence of critics in the West and the strength of his competition in the bookstores from works by novelists and poets of a postwar generation. By 1916 George Brett was telling George Macmillan that he was "aghast" at the speed with which Tagore was submitting manuscripts and expecting them to appear as books within a few months.[70] Critics were beginning to ask whether Tagore had other strings to his instrument than those sounded in *Gitanjali* and the succeeding books of poems. He did indeed, but he was even then in the process of tuning them all wrong. His first two volumes of short fiction were in process of preparation, but he left the

translations to "various hands." These were Andrews; Sister
Nivedita (Margaret Noble), who had affiliated herself with the
Ramakrishna Mission; and several Indian colleagues, who produced a dismaying variety of literary mannerisms in the translations. Charles Whibley was reader for these also. He wrote as
follows to George Macmillan:

I am sending you a formal report of Tagore's stories, because I
understand that others are coming. But meanwhile may I say that
those, which I have, are unequal, and some of them might well be
replaced by others. As to the translations, those done by C. F.
Andrews are by no means bad. A very little correction of grammatical
slips etc. would put them right. The rest, some the work of a
missionary, others the work of Indians, would require a good deal
of castigation, especially in the way of cutting out foolish Latinisms,
dear to the Babu, and of simplifying the style to the proper level.
The stories themselves are of considerable (if varying) merit, and
would doubtless be appreciated by Tagore's admirers. But, as I
said, this is an *interim* opinion, and I shall await the rest of the
material with interest.[71]

Even if allowances are made for Whibley's ignorance of the
language and for his condescending attitude toward "the Babus,"
he must again have credit for what should have been a warning to Tagore: Tagore's audience now had definite limitations;
his "admirers" would buy the books, but they would not win
many converts. That Whibley was unaware at that point of the
actual provenance of the stories he admired is borne out by a
letter from Andrews to Rothenstein, saying that Tagore had
given "far too generous an acknowledgement" in *The Hungry
Stones and Other Stories*, for Andrews did not "really translate":
he knew too little Bengali to do so, and Tagore had dictated to
him. By Tagore's explicit instructions, Macmillan entrusted selection, revision, and proof corrections of the stories to Whibley.[72]
    Similar confusion beset other aspects of production. The Lon-
don and New York firms planned simultaneous publication of
Tagore's books, and it was essential that enough copies to secure
copyright in both countries be issued on the same date in
England and in the United States. This normally complex pro-

cedure was made more so by Tagore's frequent changes of address during his travels, and by the fact that either he or his assistants still frequently countermanded his instructions given to Macmillan. The *Reminiscences* were appearing monthly in the English-language Calcutta journal *The Modern Review* before either Macmillan firm knew about this plan, which violated Tagore's contracts with them. The London firm, his agent, heard about it from George Brett in New York, who feared that, as no copyright had been filed for the Calcutta publication, an American publisher might pirate them for publication in the Unitetd States.[73]

The production of the three novels was another case in point. *The Home and the World* was Surendranath Tagore's translation, "revised by the Author."[74] The last chapter reached London in December 1918. Although correspondence was difficult in the aftermath of a war, and in the absence of international airmail service, the Macmillans were usually very efficient with respect to letter-writing. Therefore, one is struck by the paucity of letters exchanged about this book. It is not difficult, however, to understand why Tagore did not give it his undivided attention. Between mid-January and mid-March of 1919 he was lecturing in South India. Back in Bengal, he gave an important public lecture in Calcutta. Back at Santiniketan, he launched a new monthly journal, in addition to other work then in progress. In April he was deeply distressed and distracted by the declaration of martial law in the Punjab, culminating in the tragedy at Amritsar and in resignation of his knighthood on May 30. Thus the furor over these events coincided with the publication of *The Home and the World*. During the five months that must have seen the most intensive editorial work on the novel in London, its author was entirely taken up with other concerns. There is no evidence of his having even read proofs.

Macmillan correspondence reveals that *The Wreck* had been scheduled to appear first. This translation, which was being done in England, encountered so much difficulty that *The Home and the World* was ready first to go to press. George Macmillan in London wrote to George Brett of the New York firm: "As this book is ready it must of course take precedence of the longer novel which is being translated by Mr. J. D. Anderson, but that in any case is not likely to be ready for the printer for some time to come."[75]

Anderson was an admirable—and a belated—choice. He had initiated this project by proposing himself to Tagore as the translator. In September 1918 Maurice Macmillan of the London firm had proposed to George Brett that the New York firm accept this book for simultaneous publication, as "we gather from a letter of Tagore's, which Anderson encloses, that the author thinks well of Mr. Anderson's capabilities, and is inclined to encourage the enterprise."[76] Brett accepted this arrangement, and in January 1919 Anderson was at work on the translation. At the same time, George Macmillan expressed surprise that Andrews, in New York, had delivered to Brett "copy for the last chapter of this novel, for I had supposed that the complete book was in Mr. Anderson's hands."[77] This was the same book that George Macmillan one week earlier had supposed would take considerably longer to complete than *The Home and the World!* How much work Anderson was actually able to complete is not known; he died on November 20, 1920. In April 1920, however, *The Wreck* had turned up in the hands of J. G. Drummond, another retired Indian Civil Service official, in no way comparable to Anderson as linguist or literary scholar. Drummond submitted several chapters to Tagore and to Macmillan, but whether he began the work over again, or whether he took up where Anderson had left off, is unclear. Tagore rejected Drummond's chapters, unless someone could be found to give them stylistic revision. Sturge Moore was enlisted but abandoned the work when he found that "to make it much better than it is would require a great deal more time than I can possibly spare."[78] When *The Wreck* finally appeared in 1921, no translator was identified, so that literary historians, as well as reviewers, had no information at all about the provenance of the translation. Tagore wrote in April 1921 to call Macmillan's attention to the fact that no translator's name had been included and asked that this be corrected.[79] The translator's name is still missing; Macmillan was perhaps at a loss as to which translator to specify.

The circumstances of *Gora* were similar. In 1921 Tagore asked Andrews to ask Macmillan whether they would publish this novel, which he had asked Surendranath Tagore to translate. In this same letter Andrews asked Macmillan to confirm a previous refusal to publish *Cokher Bāli*, which had been translated by Surendranath for serial publication in *The Modern Review* in 1914.[80] Macmillan had indeed rejected *Cokher Bāli*, and although the translator's note in *Gora* mentions only Surendranath by name, as the person who had "corrected" the translation, it had in fact been done by W. W. Pearson, a teacher at Santiniketan. As so often in the past, Tagore, after having approved a translator, and after remaining out of touch with the editors, complained that he did not like the English translation and charged the publisher with having rushed it into publication, thereby causing it to be a failure with critics and public.[81]

It would be comforting to be able to think that prosaic concerns such as these remain remote from the realms inhabited by poets, as well as from discussions of their work. But this is a world in which practical considerations crowd closely upon the writer, and in which complexities multiply for the writer who crosses international boundaries. It is important that the record include this aspect of a writer's experience. It is especially important in the case of Tagore, not only because, in Buddhadeva Bose's words, he is a phenomenon, but also because his exchanges with the West served as paradigm for so much literary and social history that followed—and still is following—in his wake.

CHAPTER 5

Conclusion: The Inescapable Man

IN 1940 the Bengali poet Jibanananda Das said in his own way what so many other Bengali writers, before and since, have said about Rabindranath Tagore: "... we are still so close to his continuing radiance that the fixed perspective of history necessary for clear acceptance of a great poet and great man is beyond our reach." He went on to speak of the younger poets' struggles to find an identity of their own; like Buddhadeva Bose, he found it impossible to speak about breaking away from Tagore without turning back to him, if only as the point of departure: "Whatever we receive from Tagore's poetry does not attract us, because it is transmitted through an overabundance of tragic landscape, but it is more pure and valuable to us than the poetic quest of the nineteenth-century Symbolist poets or their English disciples—simply because it is touched by the great personality of Rabindranath." Rebellious younger poets experimented with the poetry of decadence, but "how awfully beautiful is the ideological incongruity between Tagore and the modernists!" In the final analysis, "the end result of this modern poetry which is now having only its beginnings, assisted and inspired by Rabindranath, will finally arrive at some completely new region after destroying the very foundation of Bengali literature and Rabindranath's works; ... As the English poets who, age after age, revolve about the centrality of Shakespeare, constantly extended themselves toward creation of a perfect circle, our poets, too, revolving around Rabindranath, will do the same."[1]

Tagore was not disturbed by efforts of such writers to break away; he was disturbed by those who slavishly and mindlessly imitated him and at the same time complained about his influ-

144

ence. He, like them, was a captive of history. No one else had been for so long so central to the development of Bengali intellectual life and so influential in its transition from the nineteenth to the twentieth century. He thought that his availability to Bengalis and to Bengali causes would remind even the superficial imitators of the direction in which he hoped Bengali culture might continue to go.

He did not always understand that his studied efforts to keep himself available to and for Bengalis and Bengali causes appeared as sheer vanity to some from other cultural backgrounds. The question of Tagore's vanity was put to Leonard Elmhirst, who as an agricultural economist might be called a "practical" man, and Elmhirst responded with the kind of reply that he thought Tagore would have given to such a question—an imaginary reply, but a true distillation of his long and intimate discussions with Tagore, at Santiniketan and in the West as well. Elmhirst wrote as follows:

Had you sat in my study here with Tagore and said to him "Are you a vain man?" I could guess his answer. "Of course," he would have said. "I have my little vanities. Tennyson looked the poet, though in the flesh I only saw his back, but how I envied him his beard! I used, when watching your leading actor in England, Sir Henry Irving, doing for instance Shakespeare, [to think] how much better I could have done it myself. I really fancied myself as an actor until the day, Leonard, when you and I stood with those Japanese professionals on the stage in Kyoto, where the three leading men of the Japanese theatre had combined to give us a performance. Remember, I said to you 'Leonard, these men are real actors.' I knew I could charm with my voice, singing or reciting in Bengali, and as a young man I loved singing the latest comic songs off your variety stage. But I could claim to suit my music to my poetry and my poetry to my music, because they emerge together. . . .

"Unfortunately no one of your British people could understand, or will ever understand, the contribution I have made to the literature of Bengali. I do not claim a position comparable to that of your great Shakespeare, who through English, is now known to the whole world, but I can say that in my poems I have played upon the whole gamut of human emotion in such a way that young people in Bengal will have to explore my poetry to achieve their

own richness of expression. My beard, my heart, my voice, my
clothes, yes, partly the artist and partly the poet in me. In Paris
the taxi men would fight each other for who would have the
privilege of driving me around. The cab men in England could
hardly conceal their smiles at this figure of fun. The Japanese
seamen on Japanese boats gave me a feeling that for them to carry
a poet on the ship was much more important than to carry the
captain, the admiral or a Royal princess. To be asked for my finger
prints on landing in California was for me the last word in degrada-
tion. For a poet to be treated as a criminal![2]

"But for witty, intelligent, cultured communication between
friends, give me the evening I spent in King's College, Cambridge.
I shall never forget it. Bertrand Russell, the philosopher, Lowes
Dickinson, political scientist, Frances Cornford, the poet, and one
or two more. How I wish I could have had such companionship in the
world of ideas, of philosophy, of poetry, or of religion in India.
That was an unforgettable evening."[3]

I leave it to you to decide what variety of vanity this really was.[4]

" 'How I wish I could have had such companionship in the
world of ideas...' ": he was a very lonely man. Buddhadeva
Bose says: "He had no rivals, and no examples of styles different from his; there was no criticism by which he could profit,
and scarcely a literary friend whom he could treat as an
equal.... And this, I think was a misfortune."[5] He was a captive
of his own genius. As Buddhadeva says: "Little things which
he did playfully, or because there was nobody else to do them,
turned out to be stages in the development of Bengali poetry."[6]
Continual awareness of such a responsibility becomes like a
physical burden. His lecture tours abroad were an economic
necessity for his school; they were also a psychological necessity
for Tagore, who was always hungry for occasions like the
memorable one at Cambridge. Behavior that appeared to be—
and was—quixotic, such as his impulsive cancellations of lecture
engagements, was the result of a cumulative exhaustion brought
on by intellectual overexcitement and sheer overwork. Critics
who have kept him on a pedestal designed for a god have done
him a disservice. When he is reduced to human scale his achievements are enhanced: it does not seem possible that one man,
even by living for eighty years, could have done so much.

It is important now that he be considered, and reconsidered, in the roles in which he saw himself. He is a literary figure, not a sociological model, although his experience and his works illuminate Indian social history. The West knew him only briefly and imperfectly. A renewed if belated effort to know him more fully would provide its own rewards.

Notes and References

Chapter One

1. On these beginnings, see S. K. Das, *Early Bengali Prose: Carey to Vidyāsāgar* (Calcutta, 1966).

2. T. B. Macaulay, "Minute on Education," quoted in *Sources of Indian Tradition*, comp. William Theodore de Bary et al., *Records of Civilization: Sources and Studies* (New York, 1958), p. 596.

3. Tagore, *My Reminiscences* (London, 1946), p. 182.

4. Quoted in *Imperfect Encounter: Letters of William Rothenstein and Rabindranath Tagore, 1911–1941*, ed. Mary M. Lago (Cambridge, Mass., 1972), p. 133. Rhys was at work on his *Rabindranath Tagore: A Biographical Study* (London, 1915).

5. See *In Praise of Krishna: Songs from the Bengali*, trans. Edward C. Dimock, Jr., and Denise Levertov (Garden City, N. Y., 1967), p. xix. On Vaishnavism, see S. K. De, *The Early History of the Vaishnava Faith and Movement in Bengal* (Calcutta, 1961).

6. Tagore, *My Reminiscences*, pp. 180–81.

7. See Eric Stokes, *The English Utilitarians and India* (Oxford, 1959), for the best discussion of this subject.

8. On Bengal's Partition politics from 1900 to 1947, see J. H. Broomfield, *Elite Conflict in a Plural Society: Twentieth Century Bengal* (Berkeley and Los Angeles, 1968).

9. On Rothenstein's connection with the India Society and with *Gitanjali*, see *Imperfect Encounter*, pp. 1–131.

10. The best biography of Tagore in English is by Krishna Kripalani, *Rabindranath Tagore: A Biography* (New York, 1962). The authorized Bengali biography is by Prabhatkumar Mukhopadhyay, *Rabindrajibani* (Life of Rabindranath), 4 vols. (Calcutta, 1960–64).

11. See *The Life and Letters of the Right Honourable Friedrich Max Müller, Edited by His Wife* (London, 1902), vol. 1, p. 38.

12. For Debendranath's own story, see *The Auto-Biography of Maharshi Devendranath Tagore*, trans. Satyendranath Tagore and Indira Devi [Chaudhuri] (London, 1914). For Rabindranath on his father, see *My Reminiscences*, pp. 67–99.

13. Tagore, "Ātmaparichay" (Self-Acquaintance), in his *Bichitrā* (Miscellany) (Calcutta, 1961), p. 310.

14. Tagore, "East and West," in *Towards Universal Man* (New York, 1961), p. 135.

15. *Ibid.*, p. 136.

16. Tagore, *My Reminiscences*, pp. 59–60.

17. Quoted in *Imperfect Encounter*, p. 216.

18. On Tagore and the Bāuls, see Edward C. Dimock, Jr., "Rabindranath Tagore—'The Greatest of the Bāuls of Bengal,'" *The Journal of Asian Studies*, 19 (1959), 33–51.

19. For a sample of the gibberish made of these unfortunate songs, see Tagore, *My Reminiscences*, p. 32.

20. In a set of graded primers for teaching Bengali to Bengali children (*Sahaj Path* [Easy Reading]), he introduced letters and sounds with rhyming couplets carefully designed to convey to learners the magic of sound and rhythm; metaphors and images of the countryside predominate in this material.

21. The current authorized edition is *Rabindra-Racanābali* (Rabindranath's Works), 27 vols. + 2 supp. (Calcutta, 1955–66).

22. Tagore, *Gitanjali* (*Song-Offerings*), first issued in a private edition by the India Society (1912), then in a trade edition by Macmillan (London and New York, 1913). William Rothenstein (1872–1945), portrait painter, lithographer, draughtsman, and influential member of the New English Art Club, was Principal of the Royal College of Art, 1920–1935.

Chapter Two

1. W. F. Thrall and A. Hibbard, *A Handbook to Literature*, rev. ed. by C. H. Holman (New York, 1960), p. 269.

2. For lists of Tagore's works published in Bengali and in English, see *Rabindranath Tagore: A Centenary Volume* (New Delhi, 1961), pp. 512–19.

3. Tagore, *Towards Universal Man*, p. 207.

4. See E. M. Forster, *A Passage to India* (New York, 1924), pp. 283–91; Lionel Trilling, *E. M. Forster* (New York, 1964), p. 173.

5. Tagore, *Collected Poems and Plays* (New York, 1956), p. 7.

6. Tagore, *Gitabitān* (Calcutta, 1960).

7. Tagore, "Sonār Kāthi," in *Rabindra-Racanābali* (Calcutta, 1964–66), vol. 18, pp. 521–24. Trans. Mary M. Lago and Tarun Gupta.

8. On these and related terms, see S. K. De, *Sanskrit Poetics as a Study of Aesthetic* (Berkeley and Los Angeles, 1963), p. 11.

9. See, for example, Buddhadeva Bose, *Tagore: Portrait of a Poet* (Bombay, 1962), pp. 33–34. Buddhadeva Bose (1908–1974),

poet, critic, playwright, author of novels and short stories, was head of the Department of Comparative Literature at Jadavpur University, West Bengal. His experience in both Asia and the West was varied, and although he was uncompromisingly Bengali, the contexts of his work were international.

10. In *Imperfect Encounter*, which includes, in addition to the letters of Tagore and Rothenstein, correspondence of their friends and associates in both India and the West.

11. Tagore, *Collected Poems*, pp. 162–63.

12. Tagore, *Rabindra-Racanābali*, vol. 11, pp. 262–63; *Gitabitān*, p. 233.

13. Although no conscious attempt has been made here to keep or to re-create the original rhyme or meter, the literal translation, in preserving the shape of Tagore's lines, keeps more of the rhythm of his Bengali poem than survived in the prose re-creations—a suggestion, perhaps, of one way in which some, if not all, of the qualities of his original texts might be made more available to those who cannot read Bengali.

14. Tagore, *My Reminiscences*, p. 202.

15. *Ibid.*, pp. 213–14.

16. *Ibid.*, pp. 217–18; Tagore, *The Religion of Man* (London, 1931), pp. 93–95. For *"Āhabānsangit"* see *Rabindra-Racanābali*, vol. 1, pp. 51–56.

17. See Edward J. Thompson, *Rabindranath Tagore: Poet and Dramatist* (London, 1926), pp. 45–46. For *"Nirjharer Sapnabhāngā"* see *Rabindra-Racanābali*, vol. 1, pp. 56–61.

18. See Kripalani, *Rabindranath Tagore*, pp. 69–71.

19. See Tagore, *My Reminiscences*, pp. 137–39.

20. Thompson, *Rabindranath Tagore: Poet and Dramatist*, p. 25.

21. *Ibid.*, p. 110. *Sonār Tori*, the volume of poems, is not to be confused with *The Golden Boat* (London, 1932), stories and poems by Tagore translated by Bhabani Bhattacharya. On a controversy concerning this book, see *Imperfect Encounter*, p. 344, note 6. For the title poem of *Sonār Tori*, see *Rabindra-Racanābali*, vol. 3, pp. 7–8.

22. See note 11 above. For another discussion of *Sonār Tori*, see Bose, *Tagore*, pp. 51–54.

23. Shelley, "Hymn to Intellectual Beauty," lines 74–77.

24. *Rabindra-Racanābali*, vol. 3, pp. 150–53.

25. Thompson, *Rabindranath Tagore: Poet and Dramatist*, p. 27.

26. See note 14 above.

27. See Thompson, *Rabindranath Tagore: Poet and Dramatist*, p. 34; Kripalani, *Rabindranath Tagore*, p. 181. For a brief explanation

of differences between "chaste" Bengali (*sādhubhāsā*) and colloquial Bengali (*calitbhāsā*), see Buddhadeva Bose, *An Acre of Green Grass* (Bombay, 1948), pp. 20–21.

28. See Thompson, *Rabindranath Tagore: Poet and Dramatist*, pp. 181–88.

29. See, for example, discussion of the poem "*Biraha*" (Separation), in Lago, "Tagore in Translation: A Case Study in Literary Exchange," *Books Abroad*, 46 (1972), 416–21.

30. See Broomfield, *Elite Conflict*, pp. 25–35.

31. See Bose, *An Acre of Green Grass*, pp. 9–10.

32. Quoted in Thompson, *Rabindranath Tagore: Poet and Dramatist*, p. 225.

33. *Ibid.*, p. 206; Bose, *Tagore*, p. 60.

34. Quoted in *Imperfect Encounter*, p. 166.

35. Kripalani, *Rabindranath Tagore*, p. 243, note 9.

36. Quoted in *Imperfect Encounter*, pp. 296–97.

37. The other three are *Sesh Saptak* (Last Octave) (1935), *Patraput* (A Cup [made of] Leaves) and *Syamāli* (Dark One) (1936).

38. *Rabindra-Racanābali*, vol. 16, p. 3.

39. For a translation, see Tagore, *Poems*, ed. Krishna Kripalani et al. (Calcutta, 1961), pp. 141–42.

40. *Ibid.*, pp. 134–40.

41. See S. K. Ghose, *The Later Poems of Tagore* (Calcutta, 1961), p. 91.

42. See *ibid.*, p. 99.

43. Transcript of Elmhirst diary, entry for February 22, 1922. L. K. Elmhirst (1893–1974) was Director, Institute of Rural Reconstruction (Sriniketan), Visva-Bharati University, West Bengal, 1921–24; Founder-President, International Conference of Agricultural Economists, 1939–53; Director, Dartington Hall Trust, Totnes, Devon. On his work with Tagore, see *Imperfect Encounter*, pp. 271–72; *Rabindranath Tagore: Pioneer in Education*, ed. L. K. Elmhirst (London, 1961).

44. On this episode, see *Rolland and Tagore*, eds. Aronson and Kripalani (Calcutta, 1945), pp. 89–96; Kripalani, *Rabindranath Tagore*, pp. 322, 327–29.

45. Unpublished letter, Elmhirst to the author, March 4, 1970. Cf. *Imperfect Encounter*, p. 304.

46. Poems for the English *Gitanjali* were selected from the Bengali *Gitānjali* (51), *Gitimālya* (17), *Naibedya* (16), *Kheyā* (11),

Sisu (3), and one each from *Cāitāli, Smaran, Kalpanā, Utsarga,* and *Achalāyatan.*

47. Tagore, *Collected Poems,* pp. 164–65.

48. *Rabindra-Racanābali,* vol. 11, p. 236.

49. See note 39 above. In *Rabindra-Racanābali,* vol. 16, pp. 76–77.

50. See *Imperfect Encounter,* pp. 44–48.

51. Unpublished letter, Tagore to E. J. Thompson, November 18, 1913. Collection of Edward P. Thompson.

52. Quoted in *Letters to Macmillan,* ed. Simon Nowell-Smith (London, 1967), pp. 291–92.

53. Some drafts and some revisions are among papers of William Rothenstein (Houghton Library, Harvard University) and of Thomas Sturge Moore (University of London Library).

54. See *Imperfect Encounter,* pp. 177–216. On other failures of communication between Tagore and Western interpreters, see Nabaneeta Sen, "An Aspect of Tagore-Criticism in the West: The Cloud of Mysticism," *Mahfil: A Quarterly of South Asian Literature,* 3 (1966), 9–23.

55. Bose, *Tagore,* p. 2.

56. *Ibid.,* p. 2.

57. *Ibid.,* p. 3.

58. *Ibid.,* p. 50.

59. *Ibid.,* p. 45.

60. *Ibid.,* p. 49. Amiya Chakravarty was Tagore's literary secretary from 1926 to 1933; since World War II he has lived in the United States and is Professor Emeritus of Comparative Oriental Religions and Literature at Boston University.

61. *Ibid.,* p. 51.

62. *Ibid.,* p. 52.

63. *Ibid.,* p. 55.

64. *Ibid.*

65. Bose, *Tagore,* p. 5.

66. Quoted in *Imperfect Encounter,* pp. 23–24.

67. Unpublished letter, Rothenstein to Shaw, July 1, 1912 (University of Texas). Tagore and Shaw finally met in May 1913.

68. On Yeats and Mohini Chatterjee, see Richard Ellmann, *The Identity of Yeats* (New York, 1964), pp. 44, 182, 217. D. N. Maitra (1878–1950) was Resident Surgeon, Mayo Hospital, Calcutta; see *Imperfect Encounter,* pp. 55, 59, 63, 80.

69. W. B. Yeats, Introduction to Tagore, *Gitanjali,* pp. vii–xxii.

70. [Unsigned notice], *The Athenaeum* (London), April 5, 1913, p. 382.

71. [Unsigned review], "Recent Verse," *The Spectator* (London), February 15, 1913, pp. 278–79.

72. On the Tagores and the Brahmo movement, see Kripalani, *Rabindranath Tagore,* p. 117.

73. [Unsigned review], "Mr. Tagore's Poems," *Times Literary Supplement,* November 7, 1912, p. 492.

74. [Unsigned review], "*Gitanjali (Song-Offerings),*" *The Athenaeum,* November 16, 1912, p. 583.

75. *Ibid.*

76. See note 70 above.

77. On Tagore in the United States, see Sujit Mukherjee, *Passage to America: The Reception of Rabindranath Tagore in the United States, 1912–1941* (Calcutta, 1964).

78. Unpublished letter, Evelyn Underhill [Mrs. Stuart Moore] to Tagore, August [19], 1913 (Rabindra-Sadana [Tagore Archives], Santiniketan). *One Hundred Poems of Kabir* (London, 1914) was later issued as *Songs of Kabir* (New York, 1915). Miss Underhill (1875–1941) was a poet as well as a student of religious mysticism. On her work with Tagore and others who translated the Kabir songs, see *Imperfect Encounter,* pp. 77, 123–25, *passim,* 154–60, 183, 188. For her unsigned review of *Gitanjali,* see *The Nation* (London), 12 (1912–13), 320–22.

79. May Sinclair (1879–1946) was an Edwardian novelist. See her "The Gitanjali: Or Song-Offerings of Rabindra Nath Tagore," *The North American Review* (New York), 197 (1913), 659–76.

80. [Unsigned review], "Romance from Bengal," *The Nation* (New York), 96 (1913), 500.

81. T. W. Rolleston (1857–1920) was First Honorary Secretary, Irish Literary Society, London, 1892–93; Assistant Editor, New Irish Library, 1893; Managing Director, Irish Industries Association, 1894–97; Honorary Secretary, Irish Arts and Crafts Society, 1899–1908; organizer, Irish loan collection for the St. Louis Exposition, 1904; Treasurer, India Society, 1910–15. See *Whitman and Rolleston: A Correspondence,* ed. Horst Frenz (Bloomington, Indiana, 1951). For his review, see "Gitanjali," *The Hibbert Journal,* 11 (1913), 693. This review was a logical result of Rothenstein's showing Tagore's manuscripts to Stopford A. Brooke (1832–1916), literary historian and theologian, who was the father-in-law of both Rolleston and L. P. Jacks, editor of *The Hibbert Journal.*

82. *Ibid.*

83. For Pound's letters about Tagore to Harriet Monroe (1860–

1936), see *The Letters of Ezra Pound* (New York, 1950), pp. 10, 13, 16, 19.

84. Pound, "Rabindranath Tagore," *The Fortnightly Review* (London), 99 (1913), 571–79.

85. For other increasingly tactless comments on Tagore, see Pound, *Letters,* pp. 21, 29, 103, 330.

86. Author's interview with Miss Stella Rhys, London, October 5, 1974. Ernest Rhys (1859–1946) edited 965 separate volumes for Everyman's Library.

87. Rhys, *Rabindranath Tagore,* p. 2.

88. Rhys, "Gitanjali," *The Nineteenth Century and After,* 73 (1913), 897–902.

89. Unpublished letter, Rhys to Tagore, September 7, 1913 (Rabindra-Sadana).

90. Unpublished letter, Rhys to Tagore, November 11, 1913 (Rabindra-Sadana).

91. Unpublished letter, Rhys to Tagore, January 1914 (Rabindra-Sadana).

92. Unpublished letter, Rhys to Tagore, February 24, 1913 (Rabindra-Sadana).

93. Unpublished letter, Rhys to Rothenstein, May 19, 1914 (Houghton Library, Harvard University).

94. Unpublished letter, Rhys to Tagore, June 5, 1914 (Rabindra-Sadana).

95. Unpublished portion of letter, Rhys to Rothenstein, June 18, 1914 (Houghton Library, Harvard University). See also *Imperfect Encounter,* p. 169, note 1. The "big book" was D. C. Sen, *History of Bengali Language and Literature,* 2nd ed. (Calcutta, 1954).

96. Unpublished letter, Rhys to Tagore, June 27, 1914 (Rabindra-Sadana).

97. See Mukherjee, *Passage to America,* pp. 24–27; B. K. Roy, *Rabindranath Tagore: The Man and His Poetry* (New York, 1915).

98. See Roy, *Rabindranath Tagore,* pp. 148, 189–94.

99. A. H. Fox Strangways (1859–1948), a teacher at Wellington College, 1887–1910; appointed music critic for *The Times,* 1911; for *The Observer,* 1925; founder-editor, *Music and Letters,* 1920–36.

100. [Unsigned review], "Tagore, India's Famous Poet and Prophet," *The New York Times Book Review,* July 25, 1915, p. 269. Cf. Roy, *Rabindranath Tagore,* pp. 174–75.

101. W. S. B., "A Master of Indian Poetry: The Life and the Poetry of Rabindranath Tagore," *Boston Evening Transcript,* June 9, 1915, Part 3, p. 4.

102. For Tagore's comment on the New Delhi incident, see *Imperfect Encounter,* p. 82.

103. [Unsigned review], "Rabindranath Tagore," *The Spectator* (London), Supplement, June 26, 1915, pp. 871–72.

104. [Unsigned review], *The Athenaeum,* June 1915, pp. 420–21.

105. Tagore, *Nationalism* (London, 1917).

106. Quoted in *Imperfect Encounter,* pp. 133, 169, note 1.

107. Quoted, *ibid.,* p. 202, note 1.

108. Unpublished letter, Rhys to Tagore, June 16, 1915 (Rabindra-Sadana).

109. Edward J. Thompson, *Rabindranath Tagore: His Life and Work* (Calcutta, 1921). E. J. Thompson (1886–1946), novelist, poet, and historian; missionary teacher in the Wesleyan Methodist Mission at Bankura, Bengal; Lecturer in Bengali, Oxford, 1922–33.

110. Bose, *An Acre of Green Grass,* p. 8; for Tagore's opinion, see *Imperfect Encounter,* pp. 321–22.

Chapter Three

1. Bose, *An Acre of Green Grass,* p. 2.

2. Sukumar Sen, *History of Bengali Literature* (New Delhi, 1960), pp. 310–11.

3. Bhudev Chaudhuri, *Bāṅglā Sāhityer Chotogalpa o Galpakori* (The Short Story and Story Writers in Bengali Literature) (Calcutta, 1962), p. 103.

4. Frank O'Connor, *The Lonely Voice* (Cleveland, 1965), p. 19.

5. William H. Peden, *The American Short Story* (Boston, 1964), p. 9.

6. The authorized edition of Tagore's short stories is *Galpaguccha* (Story Collection) (Calcutta, 1955–66), 4 vols.

7. Tagore, *"Kabir Uttor"* (Poet's Reply), quoted by the editors, *Galpaguccha,* vol. 4, p. 305.

8. Tagore, "The Postmaster," in *Mashi and Other Stories,* trans. "by various writers" (London, 1918), pp. 159–66; "The Return of Khokababu," in *The Housewarming and Other Selected Writings,* trans. Mary Lago and Tarun Gupta (New York, 1965), pp. 88–95; "The Troublemaker," *ibid.,* pp. 78–87. "The Return of Khokababu" was first published as "My Lord, the Baby," in Tagore, *The Hungry Stones and Other Stories,* trans. "by several hands" (London, 1916), pp. 73–87; this is one of the stories in this collection translated by C. F. Andrews, with Tagore as adviser.

9. Tagore, quoted by the editors, *Galpaguccha,* vol. 4, p. 310.

10. Tagore, "The Postmaster," in *Mashi and Other Stories,* pp. 159–60.

11. *Ibid.,* p. 160.

12. On this translation, see Mary M. Lago, "Tagore in Translation: A Case Study in Literary Exchange," *Books Abroad,* 46 (1972), 416–21.

13. Tagore, "The Return of Khokababu," in *The Housewarming,* p. 95.

14. Tagore, "The Troublemaker," *ibid.,* p. 87.

15. Tagore, "The Return of Khokababu," *ibid.,* p. 94.

16. Stokes, *The English Utilitarians and India,* p. 82.

17. Tagore, "The Atonement," in *The Housewarming,* pp. 57–69; "Rashmoni's Son," trans. Mary Lago and Tarun Gupta, *Chicago Review,* 19 (1966), 5–32; "The Devotée," in *The Housewarming,* pp. 151–63.

18. Tagore, "The Atonement," in *The Housewarming,* p. 59.

19. *Ibid.,* p. 62.

20. *Ibid.,* p. 66.

21. Tagore, "Rashmoni's Son," *Chicago Review,* 19 (1966), 10.

22. *Ibid.,* p. 17.

23. *Ibid.,* p. 32.

24. Tagore, "The Devotée," in *The Housewarming,* p. 153.

25. On conditions at Calcutta University, see Calcutta University Commission, *Report,* 13 vols. (Calcutta, 1919).

26. Tagore, "The Vicissitudes of Education," in *Towards Universal Man,* pp. 39–40.

27. Tagore, "A Poet's School," *ibid.,* pp. 291–92.

28. Tagore, "The Editor," in *Broken Ties and Other Stories* (translator unidentified) (London, 1925), pp. 165–75.

29. *Ibid.,* p. 171.

30. *Ibid.,* pp. 168–69. The vicissitudes of translation are illustrated by comparison with this stricter rendering: "The contents of [his paper] were quite naked. It poured out abuse so energetically in such unadulterated colloquialisms that the letters seemed to scream in your face. Therefore, the inhabitants of the two villages understood it perfectly."

31. *Ibid.,* p. 172. More strictly rendered: "The result was that even when I won, I lost in the minds of my readers. In desperation I wrote a homily on good taste. I saw that I had made a serious mistake, for it is easier to make fun of really good things than of the ridiculous. Monkeys can easily make fun of men; men who make fun of monkeys can never do it as successfully." By omitting

the analogy on men and monkeys, the translation seriously diluted the scathing tone of Tagore's original paragraph.

32. For Tagore's most concentrated fictional study of the nationalist who creates havoc in a rural setting, see his novel *The Home and the World* (*Ghare Bāire*) (London, 1916).

33. Tagore, "Cloud and Sun," in *The Runaway and Other Stories*, trans. "by various writers" (Calcutta, 1959), pp. 53–95.

34. *Ibid.*, p. 59.

35. *Ibid.*, pp. 72–73.

36. *Ibid.*, p. 70.

37. See note 26 above.

38. Tagore, " 'We Crown Thee King,' " in *The Hungry Stones and Other Stories*, pp. 215–37. *Rājtikā* means "royal mark."

39. *Ibid.*, pp. 215–16. Tagore's Bengali text says, literally, that Nabendu's "young head began to bob restlessly up and down like a pumpkin in the wind at the doors of Englishmen." The Bengali story (*Galpaguccha*, vol. 2, pp. 384–93) has many *double entendres*. "Pumpkin" is a play on the word "*kushmānda*," which means also "a false conception." Pramathanath on the train is described as "*ingrājbeshdhāri*," omitted altogether on page 218 of the translation; it means "hypocrite Englishman."

40. *Ibid.*, pp. 218–19.

41. *Ibid.*, p. 236.

42. Tagore, "*Ekrātri*," in *Galpaguccha*, vol. 1, pp. 84–89.

43. Tagore, "Broken Ties," in *Broken Ties and Other Stories*, pp. 1–126.

44. Tagore, "The Rejected Story," in *The Housewarming*, pp. 179–91.

45. For a discussion of this novel, see Kripalani, *Rabindranath Tagore*, pp. 251–53. For comments on the translation, see Lago, "Tagore in Translation," p. 420.

46. See Tagore, "Woman," in *Personality: Lectures Delivered in America* (London, 1927), pp. 169–84.

47. Tagore, "The Tutor," in *The Housewarming*, p. 122.

48. Tagore, "Bride and Bridegroom," *ibid.*, pp. 163–79.

49. *Ibid.*, p. 172.

50. Tagore, "The Girl Between," in *The Housewarming*, pp. 125–38; *The Broken Nest*, trans. Mary M. Lago and Supriya Sen (Columbia, Missouri, 1971); "A Wife's Letter," in *The Housewarming*, pp. 125–38.

51. Tagore, "The Girl Between," in *The Housewarming*, p. 47.

52. *Ibid.*, pp. 51–52.

53. *Ibid.*, p. 53.
54. *Ibid.*, p. 55.
55. *Ibid.*
56. *Ibid.*, p. 56.
57. *Ibid.*
58. *Ibid.*
59. *Ibid.*, p. 53.
60. Tagore, *The Broken Nest,* p. 78.
61. *Ibid.*, pp. 79–80.
62. *Ibid.*, p. 88.
63. *Ibid.*, p. 90.
64. Kripalani, *Rabindranath Tagore,* p. 186; Tagore, *Cokher Bāli,* trans. Krishna Kripalani, as *Binodini* (Honolulu, 1964).
65. Tagore's view of the Swadeshi extremists, as presented in *The Home and the World,* is consistent with his grounds for withdrawing from the Partition protests because he disapproved of terrorist methods: the end does not justify the means, if the means are unworthy.
66. Kripalani, *Rabindranath Tagore,* pp. 186–87.
67. Tagore, "A Wife's Letter," in *The Housewarming,* p. 126.
68. *Ibid.*, p. 125.
69. *Ibid.*
70. *Ibid.*, p. 126.
71. *Ibid.*, pp. 126–27.
72. *Ibid.*, p. 127.
73. *Ibid.*
74. *Ibid.*, p. 128.
75. *Ibid.*, p. 132.
76. *Ibid.*, p. 135.
77. *Ibid.*, p. 136.
78. *Ibid.*, pp. 136–37.
79. Tagore, "Punishment," in *The Housewarming,* pp. 35–45. For a discussion of this story, see Lago, "Modes of Questioning in Tagore's Short Fiction," *Studies in Short Fiction,* 5 (1967), 24–36.
80. Tagore, "Punishment," in *The Housewarming,* p. 38.
81. [Unsigned review], "*The Hungry Stones,*" *The Nation* (London), December 23, 1916, p. 448.
82. [Unsigned notice], *The Athenaeum,* December 1916, p. 597.
83. Edward E. Hale, "Recent Fiction," *The Dial* (New York), 61 (1916), 466–69.
84. [Unsigned review], "New Books Reviewed," *The North American Review,* 205 (1917), 149–50.

85. [Unsigned review], "Indian Tales," *Times Literary Supplement,* April 18, 1918, p. 183.

86. [Unsigned notice], *The Athenaeum,* May 1918, p. 244.

87. Edward J. O'Brien, "Some Books of Short Stories," *The Bookman* (New York), 47 (1918), 299–305.

88. [Unsigned review], "Interpretations in Little," *The Nation* (New York), May 18, 1918, p. 597.

89. Quoted in *The Living Age,* January 30, 1926, p. 260.

90. [Unsigned review], "Rabindranath Tagore," *New York Times Book Review,* October 10, 1926, p. 11.

Chapter Four

1. Tagore, *My Reminiscences,* pp. 19–20.

2. Bose, *An Acre of Green Grass,* p. 1.

3. Tagore, *Mashi and Other Stories,* pp. 3–27; *The Housewarming,* pp. 247–85.

4. *Ibid.,* pp. 215–46.

5. On *Chitrāngadā* and Tagore's sources for the story, see Kripalani, *Rabindranath Tagore,* pp. 139–43.

6. For the English verse-drama, see Tagore, *Collected Poems,* pp. 121–38.

7. Kripalani, *Rabindranath Tagore,* p. 205.

8. See *Imperfect Encounter,* p. 264, note 2; for the story, "Daliya," see *The Housewarming,* pp. 13–21.

9. See *Imperfect Encounter,* p. 23.

10. Rhys, *Rabindranath Tagore,* pp.. 79–80.

11. [Unsigned review], "An Indian Play at the Court," *The Globe* (London), July 11, 1913, p. 4.

12. [Unsigned review], "Indian Poet's Dream Play," *The Standard* (London), July 11, 1913, p. 5.

13. [Unsigned review], "An Indian Allegory: The Irish Players in a New Role," *The Evening Standard* (London), July 11, 1913, p. 6.

14. [Unsigned review], "The Irish Players," *The Times* (London), July 11, 1913, p. 8.

15. J. W., "Royal Court Theatre," *The Westminster Gazette* (London), July 11, 1913, p. 3.

16. Bose, *An Acre of Green Grass,* p. 98.

17. Bibhutibhusan Bannerji (1899–1950) based his *Pather Panchāli* (Songs of the Road) (1929) and *Aparajita* (Unconquered) (1932) on his own life story. The Bengali film director, Satyajit Ray (1922–   ) produced *Pather Panchāli* (1955), *Aparajita* (1956), and *Apur Sangshār* (The World of Apu) (1959).

18. See Chapter Two, note 15, above.

19. Sukumar Sen, *History of Bengali Literature*, p. 232. On the influence of Bankimchandra Chatterji, see also J. C. Ghosh, *Bengali Literature* (London, 1948), pp. 152–64. In 1901 Tagore, as editor, revived *Bangadarsan* (Mirror of Bengal), a monthly journal begun by Bankimchandra in 1872 as a means of fostering cultural revival through literature.

20. Bose, *An Acre of Green Grass*, p. 2.

21. Sen, *History of Bengali Literature*, pp. 233–34.

22. Both are available in English translation: *The Poison Tree*, trans. Miriam S. Knight (London, 1884); *Krishnakanta's Will*, trans. J. C. Ghosh (New York, 1962).

23. These vary greatly in length and not all can be classed as novels; *Two Sisters* is more accurately a novella.

24. Bose, "*Cokher Bāli*," in his *Rabindranath Kathāsāhitya* (Rabindranath and Belles Lettres) (Calcutta, 1962), pp. 129–32.

25. Tagore, *Binodini*, p. 243.

26. For text of the letter of resignation, see Thompson, *Rabindranath Tagore: Poet and Dramatist*, pp. 273–74.

27. See *Imperfect Encounter*, pp. 267–97.

28. [Unsigned review], "A Novel of Modern India," *The Saturday Review* (London), 127 (1919), 636.

29. [Unsigned review], "New Worlds and Old," *The Nation* (New York), 109 (1919), 153.

30. [Unsigned review], "Latest Fiction," *The New York Times*, June 8, 1919, Section 8, p. 313.

31. See Mukherjee, *Passage to America*, p. 53.

32. *Ibid.*, p. 179.

33. See Chapter Three, note 28, above.

34. E. M. F[orster], "Tagore as a Novelist," *The Athenaeum* (London), August 1, 1919, p. 687.

35. On this translation, see Lago, "Tagore in Translation," p. 420.

36. Published in 1907.

37. See Chapter Three, note 50, above.

38. Forster, "The Home and the World," *Abinger Harvest* (New York, 1936), p. 331.

39. See Mukherjee, *Passage to America*, p. 57.

40. *A Tagore Reader*, ed. Amiya Chakravarty (New York, 1961), pp 225–54.

41. See *Imperfect Encounter*, p. 226, note 4.

42. See, for example, *ibid.*, p. 19.

43. Unpublished letter, Mollie Cohen to the author, February 2, 1970.

44. Quoted in *Imperfect Encounter*, p. 226, note 4.

45. Quoted, *ibid*.

46. Unpublished letter, Tagore to Yeats, March 5, 1916. Collection of Senator Michael Yeats.

47. Tagore sent this manuscript to the London Macmillans and asked whether they thought it "of interest to your readers" (Macmillan Papers, British Library). This was edited in London by Thomas Sturge Moore; drafts with his corrections and emendations are among his papers at London University.

48. Unpublished letter, Tagore to Yeats, June 17, 1918. Collection of Senator Michael Yeats.

49. Tagore, *Russiār Cithi* (1931), trans. Sasadhar Sinha, as *Letters from Russia* (Calcutta, 1960).

50. See note 43 above.

51. Tagore, *"Landane"* (In London), in his *Pather Sancay*, in *Rabindra-Racanābali*, vol. 26, pp. 514–15.

52. Tagore, *"Bandhu"* (Friend), *ibid.*, p. 517.

53. *Ibid.*, p. 518

54. *Ibid.*, pp. 520–21.

55. *Ibid.*, p. 519.

56. Tagore, *"Landane,"* *ibid.*, pp. 515–16.

57. Tagore, *"Inglānder Bhābuksamāj"* (England's Society of Thinkers), *ibid.*, pp. 534–35.

58. Tagore, *"Stapphord Bruk"* (Stopford Brooke), *ibid.*, p. 529.

59. Tagore, *"Kabi Ietsh"* (Poet Yeats), *ibid.*, pp. 521–25.

60. Tagore, "On the Eve of Departure," in his *Towards Universal Man*, pp. 159–60.

61. See note 1 above.

62. Tagore, "On the Eve of Departure," p. 161.

63. Tagore, *Crisis in Civilization* (Calcutta, 1941).

64. Tagore, "On the Eve of Departure," p. 174.

65. See, for example, *Imperfect Encounter*, p. 211.

66. Unpublished letter, George Macmillan to Rothenstein, November 26, 1912 (Houghton Library, Harvard University).

67. For text of Whibley's report, see *Imperfect Encounter*, pp. 21–22.

68. Quoted in *Imperfect Encounter*, p. 65.

69. Unpublished letter, A. H. Fox Strangways to George Brett, January 19, 1914 (Macmillan Papers, New York Public Library).

70. Quoted in *Imperfect Encounter*, p. 221.

71. Unpublished report, Whibley to George Macmillan, February 16 [1916]. (Macmillan Papers, British Library).

72. Unpublished letter, Andrews to Rothenstein, January 8, 1917 (Houghton Library, Harvard University). Charles Freer Andrews (1871–1940), Fellow of Pembroke College, Cambridge, went to Delhi in 1904 as a missionary teacher, met Tagore in London while on home leave in 1912, and joined him at Santiniketan in 1914.

73. Unpublished letter, Brett to Sir Frederick Macmillan, March 22, 1916 (Macmillan Papers, New York Public Library).

74. Identified on the acknowledgment page as "Publishers' Note."

75. Unpublished letter, George Macmillan to Brett, January 24, 1919 (Macmillan Papers, New York Public Library).

76. Unpublished letter, Maurice Macmillan to Brett, September 19, 1918 (Macmillan Papers, New York Public Library).

77. Unpublished letter, George Macmillan to Brett, January 18, 1919 (Macmillan Papers, New York Public Library).

78. Quoted in *Imperfect Encounter,* p. 268.

79. Unpublished letter, Tagore to Macmillan, April 24, 1921 (Macmillan Papers, British Library).

80. Unpublished letter, Andrews to Macmillan, August 11, 1921 (Macmillan Papers, British Library).

81. See *Imperfect Encounter,* p. 319, note 1. W. W. Pearson (1881–1923) had served with the London Missionary Society at Bhowanipur, Calcutta. In 1912 he took a teaching post in New Delhi and in 1913 joined Tagore at Santiniketan.

Conclusion

1. Jibanananda Das, "*Rabindranāth o Ādhunik Bānglā Kabitā*" (Rabindranath and Modern Bengali Poetry), in his *Kabitār Kathā* (On Poetry) (Calcutta, 1963), pp. 19–26; trans. Deepak Majumdar and Mary M. Lago, in *Mahfil: A Quarterly of South Asian Literature,* 3 (1967), 5–10.

2. See Stephen N. Hay, "Rabindranath Tagore in America," *American Quarterly,* 14 (1962), 457–58; Mukherjee, *Passage to America,* pp. 95–99.

3. See *Imperfect Encounter,* p. 19.

4. Unpublished letter, Elmhirst to the author, October 13, 1967.

5. Bose, *Tagore,* pp. 37–38.

6. *Ibid.,* p. 64.

Selected Bibliography

PRIMARY SOURCES

1. Bengali collections:

Bicitrā (Miscellany). Calcutta: Visva-Bharati, 1961.
Galpaguccha (Story Collection). 4 vols. Calcutta: Visva-Bharati, 1960–62.
Gitabitān (Song Collection). Calcutta: Visva-Bharati, 1960.
Pather Sancay (Travel Notes). Calcutta: Visva-Bharati, 1939.
Rabindra-Racanābali (Rabindranath's Works). 27 vols., 2 supp., and index. Calcutta: Visva-Bharati, 1964–66.

2. English publications:

Binodini. Krishna Kripalani, trans. Honolulu: East-West Center Press, 1964.
The Broken Nest. Mary M. Lago and Supriya Sen, trans. Columbia, Missouri: University of Missouri Press, 1971; Madras: Macmillan India, 1974.
Broken Ties and Other Stories. London: Macmillan, 1925.
Chitra. London: The India Society, 1913; Macmillan, 1914.
Collected Poems and Plays. New York: Macmillan, 1936.
Creative Unity. London: Macmillan, 1922.
The Crescent Moon. London: Macmillan, 1913.
Crisis in Civilization. Calcutta: Visva-Bharati, 1941.
Farewell, My Friend. Krishna Kripalani, trans. London: The New India Publishing Company [1949].
Four Chapters. Surendranath Tagore, trans. Calcutta: Visva-Bharati, 1950.
Fruit-Gathering. London: Macmillan, 1916.
The Gardener. London: Macmillan, 1913.
Gitanjali (Song-Offerings). London: The India Society, 1912; Macmillan, 1913.
Glimpses of Bengal. Surendranath Tagore, trans. [revised by Thomas Sturge Moore]. London: Macmillan, 1921.
The Golden Boat. Bhabani Bhattacharya, trans. London: Allen and Unwin, 1932.

Gora [W. W. Pearson, trans., revised by Surendranath Tagore].
London: Macmillan, 1924.

The Home and the World. Surendranath Tagore, trans., revised by
the author. London: Macmillan, 1919.

The Housewarming and Other Selected Writings. Mary Lago and
Tarun Gupta, trans.; Amiya Chakravarty, ed. New York: New
American Library, 1965.

The Hungry Stones and Other Stories. London: Macmillan, 1916.

The King of the Dark Chamber. K. C. Sen, trans. London: Macmillan, 1914.

Letters from Abroad. Madras: S. Ganesan, 1924.

Letters from Russia. Calcutta: Visva-Bharati, 1960.

Letters to a Friend [*Letters from Abroad* revised and enlarged].
London: Allen and Unwin, 1928.

Lover's Gift and Crossing. London: Macmillan, 1918.

Mashi and Other Stories. London: Macmillan, 1918.

My Boyhood Days. Santiniketan: Visva-Bharati [1940].

My Reminiscences. London: Macmillan, 1917.

Nationalism. London: Macmillan, 1917.

Personality: Lectures Delivered in America. London: Macmillan, 1917.

Poems. Krishna Kripalani et al., eds. Calcutta: Visva-Bharati, 1961.

The Post Office. Devabrata Mukerjea, trans. Churchtown, Dundrum,
County Dublin: The Cuala Press, 1914.

"Rashmoni's Son," Mary Lago and Tarun Gupta, trans., *Chicago
Review,* 19 (1966), 5–32.

The Religion of Man. London: Macmillan, 1931.

The Runaway and Other Stories. Calcutta: Visva-Bharati, 1961.

Sadhana: The Realisation of Life. London: Macmillan, 1913.

A Tagore Reader. Amiya Chakravarty, ed. New York: Macmillan,
1961.

Three Plays. Marjorie Sykes, trans. Bombay: Oxford University
Press, 1950.

Towards Universal Man. Bhabani Bhattacharya, trans. and ed. New
York: Asia Publishing House, 1961.

Two Sisters. Krishna Kripalani, trans. Calcutta: Visva-Bharati, 1945.

The Wreck [J. G. Drummond, trans.]. London: Macmillan, 1921.

Manuscript Collections Cited

The British Library (British Museum), London: Macmillan Company Papers.

The Houghton Library, Harvard University: Rothenstein Papers.

The New York Public Library: Macmillan Company Papers.

Rabindra-Sadana (Tagore Archives, Santiniketan).
University of London Library: Thomas Sturge Moore Papers.
University of Texas—Austin: Humanities Research Center.

SECONDARY SOURCES

1. Books:

ARONSON, ALEX, and KRISHNA KRIPALANI, eds. *Rolland and Tagore.* Calcutta: Visva-Bharati, 1945. Letters and transcripts of conversations, 1919–1930.

BOSE, BUDDHADEVA. *An Acre of Green Grass: A Review of Modern Bengali Literature.* Calcutta: Orient Longmans, 1948. An eloquent and authoritative summary.

————. *Tagore: Portrait of a Poet.* Bombay: University of Bombay, 1962. Five lectures delivered at Bombay University in 1962.

BROOMFIELD, J. H. *Elite Conflict in a Plural Society: Twentieth-Century Bengal.* Berkeley and Los Angeles: University of California Press, 1968. Outstanding study of Bengali political history, with social ramifications, 1900–1947.

CALCUTTA UNIVERSITY COMMISSION, 1917–1919. *Report.* 13 vols. Calcutta: Superintendent Government Printing, India, 1919–20. Detailed and vivid documentation of conditions of student life in Calcutta: valuable background for Tagore's stories on this subject.

DAS, S. K. *Early Bengali Prose: Carey to Vidyāsāgar.* Calcutta: Bookland Private Ltd., 1966. Useful discussion of growth of Bengali prose in the first half of the nineteenth century.

DE, S. K. *The Early History of the Vaishnava Faith and Movement in Bengal.* Calcutta: K. L. Mukhopadhyay, 1961. Authoritative scholarly text on this subject.

————. *Sanskrit Poetics as a Study of Aesthetic.* Berkeley and Los Angeles: University of California Press, 1962. Five Tagore Memorial Lectures, University of California, 1961.

DE BARY, W. T. et al., comps. *Sources of Indian Tradition,* vol. 56: *Introduction to Oriental Civilizations.* Records of Civilization: Sources and Studies. New York: Columbia University Press, 1958. Source book covering ancient to modern times, with useful sections on the Tagores.

DIMOCK, EDWARD C., JR., and DENISE LEVERTOV, trans. *In Praise of Krishna: Songs from the Bengali.* Garden City, N. Y.: Doubleday and Co., 1967. Vaishnava `lyrics, with excellent Introduction on that movement in Bengal.

ELLMANN, RICHARD. *The Identity of Yeats.* New York: Oxford Uni-

versity Press, 1964. Exposition of Yeats's personality and background, pertinent to his interest in Tagore.

ELMHIRST, LEONARD. *Rabindranath Tagore: Pioneer in Education.*
London: John Murray, 1961. Essays on rural reconstruction
as demonstrated by Tagore and Elmhirst, and various exchanges between them.

FORSTER, E. M. *Abinger Harvest.* New York: Harcourt Brace, 1964.
Essays, including reviews of *Chitra* and *The Home and the
World.*

GHOSE, S. K. *The Later Poems of Tagore.* London: Asia Publishing
House, 1961. Most easily available book on this subject.

GHOSH, J. C. *Bengali Literature.* London: Oxford University Press,
1948. Rapid summary for Western readers, Bengali Aryan period
to Tagore.

KRIPALANI, KRISHNA. *Rabindranath Tagore: A Biography.* New
York: Grove Press, 1962. Best English biography, by a scholar
well acquainted with the Tagore family.

LAGO, MARY M., ed. *Imperfect Encounter: Letters of William
Rothenstein and Rabindranath Tagore, 1911–1941.* Cambridge,
Mass.: Harvard University Press, 1972. Correspondence, with
introductory essays on Rothenstein's role in Tagore's career and
stages in their friendship, annotated from previously unpublished
correspondence with their friends and publishers.

MUKHERJEE, SUJIT. *Passage to America: The Reception of Rabindranath Tagore in the United States, 1912–1914.* Calcutta: Bookland Private Ltd., 1964. Principally factual summary, with some
critical interpretations, of Tagore's American tours and reviewers'
reactions to his works.

RHYS, ERNEST. *Rabindranath Tagore: A Biographical Study.* London:
Macmillan, 1915. Limited biographical and critical survey,
valuable as the view of a sympathetic Western observer of the
beginning of Tagore's fame in the West.

ROTHENSTEIN, WILLIAM. *Men and Memories: Recollections of William
Rothenstein, 1900–1922.* London: Faber and Faber, 1932. Recollections of origins of the India Society, of Rothenstein's trip to
India and meetings with Tagore there and in England, and of
the launching of *Gitanjali.*

————. *Since Fifty: Men and Memories, 1922–1938.* London: Faber
and Faber, 1939. Recollections of later stages in Rothenstein-
Tagore friendship and in Rothenstein's involvement with Indian
artists.

————. *Six Portraits of Sir Rabindranath Tagore.* London: Macmillan, 1915. Portrait drawings, series begun in India in 1911.

ROY, B. K. *Rabindranath Tagore: The Man and His Poetry.* New York: Dodd, Mead, 1915. Inadequate and unsatisfactory discussion by an Indian who met Tagore in the United States.

[SAHITYA AKADEMI]. *Rabindranath Tagore: A Centenary Volume, 1861–1961.* New Delhi: Sahitya Akademi, 1961. Commemorative articles on various aspects of Tagore's life and works, with chronology and list of works.

SEN, D. C. *History of Bengali Language and Literature.* 2nd ed. Calcutta: University of Calcutta, 1954. Falls far short of present-day standards of scholarship, but an interesting Bengali view of the subject, by a writer who played a major role in preservation of Bengali folk-songs.

SEN, SUKUMAR. *History of Bengali Literature.* New Delhi: Sahitya Akademi, 1960. Useful as systematic guide to writers and principal works, with some interpretive commentary.

STOKES, ERIC. *The English Utilitarians and India.* Oxford: The Clarendon Press, 1959. Excellent detailed study of the organization of English rule in India, as influenced by Utilitarian theory and practice.

TAGORE, DEVENDRANATH. *The Auto-Biography of Maharshi Devendranath Tagore.* Trans. Surendranath Tagore and Indira Devi [Chaudhuri]. London: Macmillan, 1914. Memoirs, heavily philosophical and theological, by Tagore's father, with Introduction by Evelyn Underhill.

TAGORE, RATHINDRANATH. *On the Edges of Time.* Calcutta: Orient Longmans, 1958. Unsystematic and sometimes inaccurate memoir on life with his father.

THOMPSON, E. J. *Rabindranath Tagore: His Life and Work.* Calcutta: Y.M.C.A. Publishing House, 1921. Brief survey of Tagore and works to date, with perceptive commentary.

————. *Rabindranath Tagore: Poet and Dramatist.* London: Oxford University Press, 1926. First detailed literary study of Tagore's work in these genres, and still one of the best.

2. Articles:

DE, S. K. "Struggle of Vernaculars for Their Rightful Place in Our Universities," *Calcutta Review,* 154 (1960), 105–22. Background of an issue central to Tagore's interests.

DIMOCK, EDWARD C., JR. "Rabindranath Tagore—'The Greatest of the Bāuls of Bengal,'" *The Journal of Asian Studies,* 19 (1959), 33–51. Influence of the Bāul sect and its lyrics.

GUHA, NARESH. "Discovery of a Modern Indian Poet," *Mahfil: A Quarterly of South Asian Literature*, 3 (1966), 58–73. A Bengali scholar's analysis of Yeats's interest in Tagore.

HAY, STEPHEN. "Rabindranath Tagore in America," *American Quarterly*, 14 (1962), 439–63. An American scholar's analysis of Tagore's visits to America and repercussions thereafter.

JOSHI, UMASHANKAR. "Modernism and Indian Literature," *Indian Literature* (New Delhi), 1 (1958), 19–30. Impact of Western influences and effects of imitation and experimentation.

LAGO, MARY M. "The Essential Tagore: Missing Man in South Asian Studies," *The Journal of Commonwealth Literature* (Leeds University), 8 (1973), 81–87. Neglected primary materials on the India Society and on Tagore's career in the West.

————. "Modes of Questioning in Tagore's Short Stories," *Studies in Short Fiction*, 5 (1967), 24–36. Fictional techniques for examining Bengali social and economic problems.

————. "Restoring Rabindranath Tagore," *Encounter*, January 1974, pp. 52–57. Plea for a realistic approach to the presentation of Tagore and his works.

————. "Rothenstein, Tagore, and Bangla Desh," *The Cornhill Magazine*, Spring 1972, pp. 165–76. Examination of the West's stereotype of Tagore as wise man from the East.

————. "Tagore in Translation: A Case Study in Literary Exchange," *Books Abroad*, 46 (1972), 416–21. Explication of typical translation inaccuracies and their consequences.

POUND, EZRA. "Rabindranath Tagore," *The Fortnightly Review*, 99 (1913), 571–79. The most significant early literary evaluation of Tagore's lyrics and their sources.

————. "Rabindranath Tagore: His Second Book into English," *The New Freewoman: An Individualist Review* (London), 1 (1913), 187–88. Discussion of *The Gardener*.

SEN, NABANEETA. "An Aspect of Tagore-Criticism in the West: The Cloud of Mysticism," *Mahfil: A Quarterly of South Asian Literature*, 3 (1966), 9–23.

SENA, VINOD. "The Dilemmas of the Indian Intellectual: A Counter-Statement," *Quest* (Bombay), 26 (1960), 73–83. Reply to Shils, "The Culture of the Indian Intellectual."

SHILS, EDWARD. "The Culture of the Indian Intellectual," *Sewanee Review*, 67 (1959), 239–61, 401–21. Controversial, thought-provoking analysis of Indian intellectuals' alleged ambivalence toward modernization and Western influences.

Index

Abbey Theatre, 118, 120
Abinger Harvest (Forster), 124
Addison, Joseph, 101
Amritsar Massacre, 122, 141
Anderson, J. D., 65, 141-42
Andrews, C. F., 130, 139, 140, 142, 143, 156n8, 163n72
Aparajita (Bannerji), 160n17
"Apu novels." *See* Bannerji, Bibhutibhusan
Apur Sangshār (Bannerji), 160n17
Asiatic Society of Bengal, 28
Athenaeum, The (London), 67, 68, 77, 113, 124

Balzac, Honoré de, 87
Bangadarshan (Calcutta), 161n19
Bangladesh, 28
Bankimchandra. *See* Chatterji, Bankimchandra
Bannerji, Bibhutibhusan, 120, 160-n17
Bāuls, 31, 41, 42, 84
Bengal Academy, 32
Bengal: nationalism, 34, 77; partition, 34, 37, 50, 77, 93, 125; language, 23, 30; poetic tradition, 23-24; prose tradition, 21-22, 120
Bentham, Jeremy, 25
bhadralok, 81, 82, 87, 88, 94, 95
bhakti, 24, 31, 38
bhanitā, 47
Bhanu Singh, 48
Bishabriksha (Chatterji), 120
Blake, William, 68, 70
Boer War, 50
Bolpur. *See* Santiniketan
Bombay University, 63
Bookman, The (London), 113

Bose, Buddhadeva, 51, 63, 64, 65, 78, 80, 115, 119, 120, 121, 143, 144, 146, 150n9
Boston Evening Transcript, 77
Brahmaputra River, 56
Brahmo Samaj, 29, 67
Brett, George, 76, 139, 141, 142
Bridges, Robert, 62, 63
British Empire, 21
British Library, The (British Museum), 72
Brooke, Stopford A., 134, 136, 154-n81
Browning, Robert, 87
Buddhadeva. *See* Bose, Buddhadeva
Burke, Edmund, 96
Byron, Lord, 25, 87

Calcutta, 26, 27, 65
Calcutta University, 49, 92
Calderon, George, 117
Cambridge University, 65, 146
canzoni, 72
Carey, William, 21
Carlyle, Thomas, 87
Centenary Volume, 117
Chakravarty, Amiya, 64, 153n60
Chatterjee, Mohini, 66
Chatterji, Bankimchandra, 47, 101, 120, 121, 161n19
Chaudhuri, Bhudev, 80
Chaudhuri, Indira Devi, 128, 129
chotolok, 34, 81, 82, 94
Cicero, 96
Clive, Robert, 26
Cohen, Mollie, 127, 129
Comte, Auguste, 25
Congress. *See* Indian National Congress

171